W9-AUB-065

WORLD WAR I

GREAT
SPEECHES
IN
HISTORY

Jodie L. Zdrok,
Book Editor

Daniel Leone, *President*

Bonnie Szumski, *Publisher*

Scott Barbour, *Managing Editor*

GREENHAVEN
PRESS®

THOMSON
━━━━━✦━━━━━ ™
GALE

San Diego • Detroit • New York • San Francisco • Cleveland
New Haven, Conn. • Waterville, Maine • London • Munich

© 2004 by Greenhaven Press. Greenhaven Press is an imprint of The Gale Group, Inc., a division of Thomson Learning, Inc.

Greenhaven® and Thomson Learning™ are trademarks used herein under license.

For more information, contact
Greenhaven Press
27500 Drake Rd.
Farmington Hills, MI 48331-3535
Or you can visit our Internet site at http://www.gale.com

LIBRARY OF CONGRESS CATALOGING-IN-PUBLICATION DATA

World War I / Jodie L. Zdrok, book editor.
    p. cm. — (Greenhaven Press's great speeches in history series)
Includes bibliographical references and index.
ISBN 0-7377-1595-2 (lib. : alk. paper) — ISBN 0-7377-1596-0 (pbk. : alk. paper)
    1. World War, 1914–1918—Sources. 2. Speeches, addresses, etc. I. Title: World War 1. II. Title: World War One. III. Zdrok, Jodie L. IV. Great speeches in history series.
D511.W77 2004
940.3—dc21
                                           2003054320

Printed in the United States of America

Contents

those who oppose the war should participate in strikes and antiwar protests.

Chapter 3: Peacemaking

the war. A new international order of safety and stability is about to be established.

Foreword

I have a dream that one day this nation will rise up and live out the true meaning of its creed: "We hold these truths to be self-evident: that all men are created equal."

I have a dream that one day on the red hills of Georgia the sons of former slaves and the sons of former slave owners will be able to sit down together at the table of brotherhood.

I have a dream that one day even the state of Mississippi, a state sweltering with the heat of injustice, sweltering with the heat of oppression, will be transformed into an oasis of freedom and justice.

I have a dream that my four little children will one day live in a nation where they will not be judged by the color of their skin but by the content of their character.

Perhaps no speech in American history resonates as deeply as Martin Luther King Jr.'s "I Have a Dream," delivered in 1963 before a rapt audience of 250,000 on the steps of the Lincoln Memorial in Washington, D.C. Decades later, the speech still enthralls those who read or hear it, and stands as a philosophical guidepost for contemporary discourse on racism.

What distinguishes "I Have a Dream" from the hundreds of other speeches given during the civil rights era are King's eloquence, lyricism, and use of vivid metaphors to convey abstract ideas. Moreover, "I Have a Dream" serves not only as a record of history—a testimony to the racism that permeated American society during the 1960s—but it is also a historical event in its own right. King's speech, aired live on national television, marked the first time that the grave injustice of racism was fully articulated to a mass audience in a way that was both logical and evocative. Julian Bond, a fellow participant in the civil rights movement and student of King's, states that

> King's dramatic 1963 "I Have a Dream" speech before the Lincoln Memorial cemented his place as first among equals in civil rights leadership; from this first televised mass meeting, an American audience saw and heard the unedited oratory of America's finest preacher, and for the first time, a mass white audience heard the undeniable justice of black demands.

Moreover, by helping people to understand the justice of the civil rights movement's demands, King's speech helped to transform the nation. In 1964, a year after the speech was delivered, President Lyndon B. Johnson signed the Civil Rights Act, which outlawed segregation in public facilities and discrimination in employment. In 1965, Congress passed the Voting Rights Act, which forbids restrictions, such as literacy tests, that were commonly used in the South to prevent blacks from voting. King's impact on the country's laws illustrates the power of speech to bring about real change.

Greenhaven Press's Great Speeches in History series offers students an opportunity to read and study some of the greatest speeches ever delivered before an audience. Each volume traces a specific historical era, event, or theme through speeches—both famous and lesser known. An introductory essay sets the stage by presenting background and context. Then a collection of speeches follows, grouped in chapters based on chronology or theme. Each selection is preceded by a brief introduction that offers historical context, biographical information about the speaker, and analysis of the speech. A comprehensive index and an annotated table of contents help readers quickly locate material of interest, and a bibliography serves as a launching point for further research. Finally, an appendix of author biographies provides detailed background on each speaker's life and work. Taken together, the volumes in the Greenhaven Great Speeches in History series offer students vibrant illustrations of history and demonstrate the potency of the spoken word. By reading speeches in their historical context, students will be transported back in time and gain a deeper understanding of the issues that confronted people of the past.

Introduction:
A New World Order

"**A** tiny clipping from a newspaper, mailed without comment from a secret band of terrorists in Zagreb, capital of Croatia, to their comrades in Belgrade, was the torch which set the world afire with war in 1914. That bit of paper wrecked old, proud empires. It gave birth to new, free nations."[1]

The bit of paper, as described by Borijove Jevtic, was a message instructing the terrorists to kill Archduke Ferdinand of Austria-Hungary during his visit to Sarajevo, Bosnia, on June 28, 1914. Jevtic was a member of the Serbian terrorist group the Black Hand, which plotted the attack. The assassination took place that day as planned as Black Hand member Gavrilo Princip shot both Archduke Ferdinand and his wife Sophie to death. This act is the event that triggered the start of World War I.

The Austro-Hungarian Empire had formed in 1867 when Austria unified with Hungary. The compromise with Hungary created what became known as the dual monarchy, containing the two kingdoms of Austria and Hungary. The two kingdoms shared one king but had separate constitutions and parliaments. By 1914, the Austro-Hungarian Empire, in which fifteen different languages were spoken, contained a population of almost 50 million people.

The Austrian archduke's assassination was the culmination of a struggle between Austria-Hungary and the minorities within its widespread, multinational empire. Southern Slav groups such as the Serbians and the Croats had an active history of nationalism in the decades leading up to the war. These groups opposed the Habsburgs, the rulers of the empire and a family whose dynasty had reigned in Austria since the thirteenth century.

The assassination of Ferdinand, the Habsburg who was heir to the throne, had far-reaching effects. Initially it led to a diplomatic clash between Austria-Hungary and the Serbian government, which Austria-Hungary believed supported the terrorists. The conflict quickly escalated into a world war because the European powers honored alliances they had created with one another in the decades before the war. The Triple Alliance, consisting of Austria-Hungary, Germany, and Italy, had engaged in diplomacy with the Triple Entente, composed of Russia, France, and Great Britain. In the event of war, the members of an alliance were to come to the aid of other nations within the alliance. When diplomacy failed in the summer of 1914, one nation declared war on another. The complex chain of events unraveled as follows: On July 28, Austria-Hungary declared war on Serbia. On August 1, Germany, allied to Austria-Hungary, declared war on Russia, which viewed itself as a protector of Serbia and had begun to mobilize its armies. In response to French mobilization, Germany also declared war on France on August 3. On August 4, Germany initiated the fighting of World War I by invading Belgium, and Great Britain responded by declaring war on Germany. In sum, by August 1914, the Triple Alliance (minus Italy, which remained neutral) became the Central Powers engaged in war against the Triple Entente, or Allied Powers. The war's outbreak was described somberly by British foreign secretary Sir Edward Grey, when he remarked, "The lamps are going out all over Europe. We shall not see them lit again in our lifetime."[2] Indeed, the symbolic lamps were lit again, but only after much death, suffering, and destruction.

Most of the fighting took place on European battlefields and surrounding seas. However, the struggle is considered a "world war" because it involved nations throughout the world. For example, Turkey joined the Central Powers, while Japan and the United States entered on the side of the Allied Powers. African and South American colonies and dominions held by the Europeans also became theaters of war. More than thirty nations were involved in World War I.

The Allied Powers emerged victorious, but a heavy price

was paid by all the nations. When the fighting stopped on November 11, 1918, about 8.5 million soldiers were dead, 21 million wounded, and 7.7 million imprisoned or missing. Starvation and the poor living conditions brought on by the war caused many more people—mostly civilians—to suffer or perish.

The staggering loss of life, human suffering, and material devastation at the close of the war prompted a number of changes both within nations and in their relationships with one another. Many of these changes were expressed in the Versailles treaty, which was the product of six months of negotiations at the Paris Peace Conference at the end of the war.

The conference was heavily influenced by U.S. president Woodrow Wilson's "Fourteen Points," an articulation of American war aims and goals for peace that were later incorporated into the peace settlements. Wilson's major points included open covenants of peace, freedom of navigation on the seas, a reduction of armaments worldwide, autonomy for the peoples of Austria-Hungary, the establishment of an independent Polish state, and the creation of the League of Nations, a general association of nations designed to guarantee the political independence and territorial integrity of all nations.

Some of the provisions of the Versailles treaty were based on Wilson's Fourteen Points, and others were devised by the French and British delegates to the peace conference. The Versailles treaty consisted of the following provisions: the disarmament of Germany, reparations payments by Germany, the re-creation of Poland, the formation of nations from the defunct Austro-Hungarian Empire, a ban on the union of Germany and Austria, and the creation of the League of Nations.

The league was designed as an international governing organization that would settle disputes among nations. The League of Nations was a controversial notion in the United States. Many members of the U.S. Congress disliked the idea of an international league because they did not want America's involvement in issues abroad to interfere with either domestic affairs or sovereign power. Wilson and the League of Nations' supporters campaigned for popular endorsement, but the league's opponents emerged victorious in this strug-

Government officials gather in the Hall of Mirrors to witness the signing of the Treaty of Versailles. The peace treaty officially ended World War I.

gle. America neither joined the organization nor ratified the Versailles treaty itself.

The nations of the world thus charted a new course after the war. The challenge in the postwar era was to fashion a new world order. In the decade or so following World War I, at least three kinds of developments contributed to the establishment of this new world order. First, many countries were reconfigured following the breakup of territories. Second, some nations altered their political landscape by modifying the government and its institutions. Last, the postwar era witnessed new kinds of international cooperation through structures such as global associations and conferences.

New Nations

In the aftermath of the First World War, the map of Europe was redrawn. Some nations experienced territorial gains, while others relinquished land to existing or newly formed countries. When the Polish, Hungarian, Czech, and Slovakian segments of the population declared themselves independent from the Austro-Hungarian Empire in October 1918, nearly all that remained of the empire was German-speaking Austria. Several new nations then emerged from the remnants of the empire. These were created based on the idea of national self-determination. In practice, this meant that some of the new territorial borders were fixed according to ethnic boundaries. Three countries formed in the postwar period on the basis of national self-determination were Poland, Czechoslovakia, and Yugoslavia.

Poland was reconstituted as a nation on November 18, 1918, 123 years after it had been partitioned out of existence by Prussia, Russia, and Austria. Many political leaders shared the opinion that the partitions of Poland had been unjust acts that needed to be rectified. The defeat of Germany and Austria-Hungary made the reestablishment of Poland possible. The injustice of the partitions, coupled with the principle of self-determination, is what motivated the Allied Powers and their associates to re-create Poland.

Poland was a nation that had disappeared from the map of Europe in 1792 and was reconstituted in 1918. Czechoslovakia, on the other hand, became part of European geography for the first time in the wake of World War I. When the war broke out in 1914, two ethnic groups, the Czechs and the Slovaks, pushed for independence from the Austro-Hungarian Empire. Despite having separate histories and cultures, they worked together to break away from the empire. On October 28, 1918, the Czechs proclaimed independence from Austria-Hungary. The Slovaks seceded from Hungary two days later. The union of Slovakia and the Czech lands was proclaimed on November 14, 1918, and "Czechoslovakia" was born. The new nation, created as a parliamentary democracy, consisted of 13.6 million people. Together, the Czechs and the Slovaks made up 64 percent of the population; the rest consisted of Moravians, Ruthenians, and Germans. Despite the eventual proliferation of political parties along ethnic lines, Czechoslovakia was the most democratic nation in the region during this time.

Another multinational state emerged with the creation of Yugoslavia on December 1, 1918. Initially called the Kingdom of the Serbs, Croats, and Slovenes, after three of the largest ethnic groups comprising the new nation, the country was eventually renamed "Yugoslavia" (meaning "South Slav" Kingdom). Other groups, both Slav and non-Slav, within the borders included Macedonians, Germans, Albanians, Hungarians, Romanians, Turks, Slovaks, Ruthenians, Russians, Poles, and Bulgarians. Most of these nationalities had separate histories reaching back over a thousand years, and integration was problematic from the kingdom's inception. Although the idea of pan-Slavism, or unity among Slavic peoples, was the founding principle of the Yugoslavian state, there were too many competing interests among the nationalities for stability to be achieved. It proved to be the most unstable of the new nations in the postwar era.

After most of the Austro-Hungarian Empire had been carved into new nations, only the Austrian and Hungarian lands remained. They became separate nations after the war and collapse of the empire.

In Austria, the end of the monarchy and of the Habsburg dynasty occurred when Emperor Charles I abdicated the throne in November 1918. Austria was proclaimed a republic, and its new, reduced borders were fixed by a November 1919 treaty. In addition to territorial regulations, Austria also faced political consequences after the war. One of the Versailles treaty's provisions in the peace settlement was that Austria was forbidden to form a political or economic union with Germany without the approval of the League of Nations.

Hungary became a small country after the dissolution of the empire. It lost 71 percent of its territory and 63 percent of its population. Whereas 8 million people lived in the reconfigured Hungarian state, another 3.5 million Hungarians were left outside the newly established borders. With the collapse of the dual monarchy and the forced departure of King Charles IV after World War I, Hungary became a kingdom without a king. The commander in chief of the Austro-Hungarian navy, Admiral Miklós Horthy de Nagybánya, was made regent and remained in that role for the next twenty-five years.

It is clear that the end of World War I rendered significant shifts in the European landscape. Boundaries were redefined, ethnic groups experienced freedom and independence, and

Europe During World War I

Europe After World War I

nations coped with the geographical and political changes that hardly seemed possible just four years previously.

Political Transformations

Along with geopolitical changes, the immediate postwar world saw the emergence of new types of government in many countries. While some nations began to develop into democracies, others were becoming authoritarian regimes. Two examples of countries that underwent political transformation as a result, at least in part, of World War I are Germany and Russia.

Unified as a nation in 1871, Germany was a constitutional monarchy until the closing days of World War I. Trouble for Kaiser William II, the country's monarch, peaked when workers and troops protested the government's reluctance to end the war, and a revolution ensued. As a result, the kaiser abdicated the throne on November 9, 1918. A provisional government was in place until February 1919, when the National Assembly formed a constitution. Then, from 1918 to 1933, Germany became a democratic republic. The Germany of these years is often referred to as the Weimar Republic, named after the city in which the constitution was devised. Postwar Germany became one of the most politically free nations in the world.

It is important to note that Germany had its share of problems in the aftermath of World War I. The Versailles treaty imposed heavy reparations on Germany and took away its prewar African colonies as well as some economically significant territories. The architects of the peace treaty also placed a burden of guilt on Germany by including a clause that stated that Germany alone was responsible for the war. These elements of the Treaty of Versailles took a collective economic and psychological toll on the nation. The frustrations of the German people were made manifest through rival, increasingly factional political parties. These political struggles contributed to the republic's rapid downfall as well as to the rise of Nazism. Thus the outcome of World War I created the conditions that would ultimately lead to World War II.

In Russia, World War I amplified existing political and

societal tensions. The Russian monarchy, in the years before the war, had struggled to maintain power while meeting the demands of discontented segments of the population, including workers, peasants, and landowners. Revolutionary sentiment stirred Russia in the prewar years, but the outbreak of war initially swept those sentiments aside. Ultimately, World War I proved to be a catalyst for revolution. As French historian Elie Halévy noted, "Revolutionary emotions . . . were only submerged for a time, not annihilated; they were soon to come to the surface again, with an intensity increased by the sufferings of the War."[3]

Russia experienced a dramatic upheaval when revolution broke out in February 1917. A provisional government took over, and Czar Nicholas II abdicated. In November, the Bolsheviks, a radical Communist group led by Vladimir Lenin, seized power from the provisional government. Russia remained turbulent and plunged into civil war between 1918 and 1921. The Communist regime was victorious, and Russia (now the Soviet Union) experienced one-party rule and a radically centralized government. Party leader Lenin ruled Russia until his death in 1924. After some Communist Party infighting, Joseph Stalin emerged as the leader and remained in power until his death in 1953.

Germany and Russia are two examples of countries whose governments were transformed in the postwar period. The duration of the changed political structure in each country differed greatly. In the Soviet Union, the Communists remained in power until 1991. In Germany, however, democracy came to an end when Adolf Hitler came to power in 1933. Although the war was not the sole cause of the political transformations, it was certainly the most significant catalyst for change.

International Cooperation

Another way in which the war changed the international scene was the development of a spirit of cooperation among nations. The tremendous devastation of the First World War fostered a commitment by some leaders and nations to ensure peace in the years immediately following the war. Historian John Milton Cooper Jr. writes that President Wilson's intentions for the existence and significance of the League of Nations were based on a determination

> to prevent a recurrence of the carnage that had raged from 1914 to 1918. Even without seeing it with his own eyes, he grasped how death-dealing and calamitous modern industrial-technological warfare had become. He also recognized that death and wounding and destruction did not comprise the sum of this kind of war's evil effects. He saw that order had broken down not only among nations but also within them, releasing terrible passions that might feed into lurid ideologies.[4]

Wilson was among those who believed that negotiation and diplomacy, rather than hostile and militaristic means, should be the tactics of choice for resolving most conflicts. Countries worked toward conciliation by creating organizational bodies of arbitration as well as international conferences on armaments limitations, reparations, border disputes, and other cross-national concerns.

The most notable example of international cooperation in the postwar period was the League of Nations, which officially came into existence in April 1919 at the Paris Peace Conference. Great Britain, France, Italy, and Japan were among the major Allied powers who became members of the league. Germany and the Soviet Union were not initially members but briefly became such in the interwar period. The League of Nations had some successes with border disputes but was not able to prevent World War II.

Numerous international agreements and conferences took place in the decade or so after World War I. A few serve to illustrate the spirit of cooperation some nations shared. For example, the Washington Conference on Limitations of Naval Armaments (1921–1922), involving the United States, Great Britain, France, and Japan, limited the naval arms race and worked out agreements in the Pacific region. In Europe, border disputes and mutual guarantees were settled by the Locarno Treaty (1925), which was signed by seven nations. Foreign ministers Gustav Stresemann of Germany and Aristide Briand of France received the Nobel Peace Prize in 1926 for their efforts in this treaty. International agreements were also reached concerning financial obligations. The Dawes Plan (1924)—whose authors also received the Nobel Peace Prize—and the Young Plan (1929–1930) both addressed reparations concerns and made Germany's war debt payments to its former enemies more manageable. Last, the Kellogg-Briand Pact (1928), signed by the United States and France, was a statement of renunciation of war as a national policy. Together, these international agreements demonstrated a willingness to address grievances, voice concerns, and acknowledge competing interests in a manner that sought as its resolution peaceful negotiation and compromise.

A New World Order

A revised map of Europe, transformations of governments, and cooperation among nations helped to define a new world order after the Great War. Many believed that with the new political developments on the international scene, in the future it would be possible to avoid major wars. However, some, like British war poet Robert Graves, were skeptical that war would ever cease: "Wars don't change except in name; / The next one must go just the same, / And new foul tricks unguessed before / Will win and justify this War."[5] Indeed, World War I was not the war to end all wars, as President Wilson had wished. In little more than twenty years, the world would be at war again.

Notes

1. Borijove Jevtic, "The Assassination of Archduke Franz Ferdinand," June 1914. www.lib.byu.edu.

2. Edward Grey of Fallodon, *Twenty-Five Years: 1892–1916*, vol. 2. New York: Frederick A. Stokes, 1925, p. 20.

3. Elie Halévy, *The World Crisis of 1914–1918: An Interpretation*. Oxford: Clarendon Press, 1930, p. 41.

4. John Milton Cooper Jr., *Breaking the Heart of the World: Woodrow Wilson and the Fight for the League of Nations*. Cambridge: Cambridge University Press, 2001, p. 432.

5. Robert Graves, "The Next War," in *World War One British Poets*, ed. Candace Ward. Mineola, NY: Dover, 1997, p. 45.

CHAPTER
ONE

Europe Goes to War

The Kaiser Calls for War

Wilhelm II

The episode that led to the outbreak of World War I occurred on June 28, 1914. On that day, Gavrilo Princip of
the Serbian anarchist group the Black Hand assassinated
the Austrian archduke Francis Ferdinand and his wife,
Sophie, during their visit to Sarajevo, Bosnia. This event
triggered a number of complicated diplomatic crises involving two sets of allies: Germany and Austria-Hungary
on one side, and Russia, Britain, and France on the other.
Negotiations for peace were brief and unsuccessful, and
Germany's declarations of war ensued soon after the
peace talks. In the midst of this failing diplomacy and the
movement toward war, German kaiser (king) Wilhelm II
made the following three short speeches before the German people. The first, made from the Royal Palace balcony in Berlin on July 31, 1914, reveals the kaiser's belief
that Germany is being forced into war. The second
speech, delivered on August 1, 1914, also from the Royal
Palace, is Wilhelm's expression of thanks for the German
people's loyalty and unity on the day Germany declared
war on Russia. On August 3, Germany declared war on
France. Several weeks after the war began, the kaiser
gave another speech, the final one excerpted here, on August 18, 1914. Delivered to the guards at Potsdam, this
address served to encourage and show confidence in Germany's soldiers. Together, these three speeches reflect the
attitude of Germany's leader about the approach of war.
The kaiser did very little public speaking throughout the
war and became virtually silent in the public arena at the

Wilhelm II, "Wilhelm II's War Speeches," www.lib.byu.edu/~rdh, July/August 1914.

war's end. Wilhelm II abdicated the throne in November 1918 and later recounted his wartime experiences in a memoir.

Speech from the balcony of the Royal Palace, Berlin, July 31, 1914:

A momentous hour has struck for Germany. Envious rivals everywhere force us to legitimate defense. The sword has been forced into our hands. I hope that in the event that my efforts to the very last moment do not succeed in bringing our opponents to reason and in preserving peace, we may use the sword, with the help of God, so that we may sheathe it again with honor. War will demand enormous sacrifices by the German people, but we shall show the enemy what it means to attack Germany. And so I commend you to God. Go forth into the churches, kneel down before God, and implore his help for our brave army.

Speech from the balcony of the Royal Palace, Berlin, August 1, 1914:

I thank you from the bottom of my heart for the expression of your loyalty and your esteem. When it comes to war, all parties cease and we are all brothers. One or another party has attacked me in peacetime, but now I forgive them wholeheartedly. If our neighbors do not give us peace, then we hope and wish that our good German sword will come victorious out of this war!

Speech of Wilhelm II to the guards at Potsdam, August 18, 1914:

Former generations as well as those who stand here today have often seen the soldiers of the First Guard Regiment and My Guards at this place. We were brought together then by an oath of allegiance which we swore before God. Today all have gathered to pray for the triumph of our weapons, for now that oath must be proved to the last drop of blood. The sword, which I have left in its scabbard for decades, shall decide.

I expect My First Guard Regiment on Foot and My Guards to add a new page of fame to their glorious history. The celebration today finds us confident in God in the Highest and remembering the glorious days of Leuthen, Chlum, and St. Privat. Our ancient fame is an appeal to the German people and their sword. And the entire German nation to the last man has grasped the sword. And so I draw the sword which with the help of God I have kept in its scabbard for decades.

The sword is drawn, and I cannot sheathe it again without victory and honor. All of you shall and will see to it that only in honor is it returned to the scabbard. You are my guaranty that I can dictate peace to my enemies. Up and at the enemy! Down with the enemies of Brandenburg! Three cheers for our army!

Britain Is Obligated to Go to War

Sir Edward Grey

Sir Edward Grey served as Great Britain's foreign secretary twice in his career, first from 1892 to 1895 and then again between 1905 and 1916. In the following speech to the British House of Commons (Parliament), Grey reveals the complex elements involved in the diplomatic efforts in the summer of 1914, from the Austrian archduke's assassination on June 28 to Germany's declaration of war on Russia on August 1. Britain was a key player in the diplomacy and had the option to remain neutral or support its allies, France and Russia. This address outlines the factors influencing the British government's decision to engage in war, which it eventually did on August 4. The reasons for this are found in the two aspects of British foreign policy that were challenged by the events of the summer: The first was Great Britain's existing alliance with France and Russia, which stated that, in the event of war, each would come to the aid of the others. The second was a nineteenth-century treaty guaranteeing Belgian neutrality. Citing the alliance with France and Belgian neutrality as "obligations of honor," Grey maintained that Great Britain had no alternative but to join France in its war against Germany. On August 3, the same day that Grey delivered this speech before the British Parliament, Germany declared war on France. The following day, Germany invaded Belgium in order to launch an attack on France.

Sir Edward Grey, speech before the House of Commons, August 3, 1914.

L ast week I stated that we were working for peace not only for this country, but to preserve the peace of Europe. To-day events move so rapidly that it is exceedingly difficult to state with technical accuracy the actual state of affairs, but it is clear that the peace of Europe cannot be preserved. Russia and Germany, at any rate, have declared war upon each other.

We Have Worked to Secure Peace

Before I proceed to state the position of his Majesty's [King George V] Government I would like to clear the ground so that, before I come to state to the House what our attitude is with regard to the present crisis, the House may know exactly under what obligations the government is, or the House can be said to be, in coming to a decision on the matter. First of all, let me say, very shortly, that we have consistently worked with a single mind, with all the earnestness in our power, to preserve peace. The House may be satisfied on that point. We have always done it. During these last years, as far as his Majesty's Government is concerned, we would have no difficulty in proving that we have done so. Throughout the Balkan crisis, by general admission, we worked for peace. The cooperation of the great powers of Europe was successful in working for peace in the Balkan crisis. It is true that some of the powers had great difficulty in adjusting their points of view. It took much time and labor and discussion before they could settle their differences, but peace was secured, because peace was their main object, and they were willing to give time and trouble rather than accentuate differences rapidly.

In the present crisis it has not been possible to secure the peace of Europe: because there has been little time, and there has been a disposition—at any rate in some quarters on which I will not dwell—to force things rapidly to an issue, at any rate to the great risk of peace, and, as we now know, the result of that is that the policy of peace as far as the great powers generally are concerned is in danger. I do not want to dwell on that, and to comment on it, and to say where the blame seems to us lie, which powers were most in favor of peace, which were most disposed to risk war or endanger peace, because I would like the House to approach this crisis in which we are now from the point of view of British interests, British honor, and British obligations, free from all passion as to why peace has not yet been preserved.

The situation in the present crisis . . . has originated in a dispute between Austria and Serbia. I can say this with the most absolute confidence—no government and no country has less desire to be involved in war over a dispute with Austria than the country of France. They are involved in it because of their obligation of honor under a definite alliance with Russia. Well, it is only fair to say to the House that that obligation of honor cannot apply in the same way to us. We are not parties to the Franco-Russian alliance. We do not even know the terms of the alliance. So far I have, I think, faithfully and completely cleared the ground with regard to the question of obligation.

Obligation and Not Neutrality

I now come to what we think the situation requires of us. For many years we have had a long-standing friendship with France. I remember well the feeling in the House and my own feeling—for I spoke on the subject, I think, when the late Government made their agreement with France—the warm and cordial feeling resulting from the fact that these two nations, who had had perpetual differences in the past, had cleared these differences away; I remember saying, I think, that it seemed to me that some benign influence had been at work to produce the cordial atmosphere that had made that possible. But how far that friendship entails obligation—it has been a friendship between the nations and ratified by the nations—how far that entails an obligation, let every man look into his own heart, and his own feelings, and construe the extent of the obligation for himself. I construe it myself as I feel it, but I do not wish to urge upon any one else more than their feelings dictate as to what they should feel about the obligation. The House, individually and collectively, may judge for itself. I speak my personal view, and I have given the House my own feeling in the matter. The French fleet is now in the Mediterranean, and the northern and western coasts of France are absolutely undefended.

The French fleet being concentrated in the Mediterranean, the situation is very different from what it used to be, because the friendship which has grown up between the two countries has given them a sense of security that there was nothing to be feared from us. My own feeling is that if a foreign fleet, engaged in a war which France had not sought, and in which she had not been the aggressor, came down the English Channel and bombarded and battered the undefended coasts of France, we could not stand aside and see this going on practically within sight of our eyes, with our arms folded, looking on dispassionately, doing nothing. I believe that would be the feeling of this country. There are times when one feels that if these circumstances actually did arise, it would be a feeling which would spread with irresistible force throughout the land.

But I also want to look at the matter without sentiment, and from the point of view of British interests, and it is on that that I am going to base and justify what I am presently going to say to the House. If we say nothing at this moment, what is France to do with her fleet in the Mediterranean? If she leaves it there, with no statement from us as to what we will do, she leaves her northern and western coasts absolutely undefended, at the mercy of a German fleet coming down the Channel to do as it pleases in a war which is a war of life and death between them. If we say nothing, it may be that the French fleet is withdrawn from the Mediterranean. We are in the presence of a European conflagration; can anybody set limits to the consequences that may arise out of it? Let us assume that to-day we stand aside in an attitude of neutrality, saying, "No, we cannot undertake and engage to help either party in this conflict." Let us suppose the French fleet is withdrawn from the Mediterranean; and let us assume that the consequences—which are already tremendous in what has happened in Europe even to countries which are at peace—in fact, equally whether countries are at peace or at war—let us assume that out of that come consequences unforeseen, which make it necessary at a sudden moment that, in defense of vital British interests, we shall go to war; and let us assume which is quite possible—that Italy, who is now neutral—because, as I understand, she considers that this war is an aggressive war, and the Triple Alliance being a defensive alliance her obligation did not arise let us assume that consequences which are not yet foreseen and which, perfectly legitimately consulting her own interests, make Italy depart from her attitude of neutrality at a time when we are forced in defense of vital British interest ourselves to fight—what then will be the position in the Mediterranean? It might be that at some critical moment those consequences would be forced upon us because our trade routes in the Mediterranean might be vital to this country. . . .

Germany's Ultimatum to Belgium

It now appears from the news I have received today—which has come quite recently, and I am not yet quite sure how far it has reached me in an accurate form—that an ultimatum has been given to Belgium by Germany, the object of which was to offer Belgium friendly relations with Germany on condition that she would facilitate the passage of German troops through Belgium. Well, Sir, until one has these things absolutely definite, up to the last moment I do not wish to say all that one would say if one were in a position to give the House full, complete and absolute information upon the point. We were sounded in the course of last week as to whether, if a guarantee were given that, after the war, Belgian integrity would be preserved, that would content us. We replied that we could not bargain away whatever interests or obligations we had in Belgian neutrality.

Shortly before I reached the House I was informed that the following telegram had been received from the King of the Belgians by our King—King George:

"Remembering the numerous proofs of your Majesty's friendship and that of your predecessors, and the friendly attitude of England in 1870, and the proof of friendship she has just given us again, I make a supreme appeal to the diplomatic intervention of your Majesty's Government to safeguard the integrity of Belgium."

Diplomatic intervention took place last week on our part.

What can diplomatic intervention do now? We have great and vital interests in the independence—and integrity is the least part—of Belgium. If Belgium is compelled to submit to allow her neutrality to be violated, of course the situation is clear. Even if by agreement she admitted the violation of her neutrality, it is clear she could only do so under duress. The smaller States in that region of Europe ask but one thing. Their one desire is that they should be left alone and independent. The one thing they fear is, I think, not so much that their integrity but that their independence should be interfered with. If in this war, which is before Europe, the neutrality of those countries is violated, if the troops of one of the combatants violate its neutrality and no action be taken to resent it, at the end of war, whatever the integrity may be, the independence will be gone.

No, Sir, if it be the case that there has been anything in the nature of an ultimatum to Belgium, asking her to compromise or violate her neutrality, what ever may have been offered to her in return, her independence is gone if that holds. If her independence goes, the independence of Holland will follow. I ask the House from the point of view of British interests to consider what may be at stake. If France is beaten in a struggle of life and death, beaten to her knees, loses her position as a great power, becomes subordinate to the will and power of one greater than herself consequences which I do not anticipate, because I am sure that France has the power to defend herself with all the energy and ability and patriotism which she has shown so often—still, if that were to happen and if Belgium fell under the same dominating influence, and then Holland, and then Denmark, then would not Mr. William Gladstone's [an influential British politician who was prime minister from 1870 to 1874] words come true, that just opposite to us there would be a common interest against the unmeasured aggrandizement of any power?

It may be said, I suppose, that we might stand aside, husband our strength, and that, whatever happened in the course of this war, at the end of it intervene with effect to put things right, and to adjust them to our own point of view. If, in a crisis like this, we run away from those obligations of honor and interest as regards the Belgian treaty, I doubt whether, whatever material force we might have at the end, it would be of very much value in face of the respect that we should have lost. And I do not believe, whether a great power stands outside this war or not, it is going to be in a position at the end of it to exert its superior strength. For us, with a powerful fleet, which we believe able to protect our commerce, to protect our shores, and to protect our interests, if we are engaged in war, we shall suffer but little more than we shall suffer even if we stand aside.

We are going to suffer, I am afraid, terribly in this war, whether we are in it or whether we stand aside. Foreign trade is going to stop, not because the trade routes are closed, but because there is no trade at the other end. Continental nations engaged in war all their populations, all their energies, all their wealth, engaged in a desperate struggle they cannot carry on the trade with us that they are carrying on in times of peace, whether we are parties to the war or whether we are not. I do not believe for a moment that at the end of this war, even if we stood aside and remained aside, we should be in a position, a material position, to use our force decisively to undo what had happened in the course of the war, to prevent the whole of the west of Europe opposite to us—if that had been the result of the war—falling under the domination of a single power, and I am quite sure that our moral position would be such as to have lost us all respect. I can only say that I have put the question of Belgium somewhat hypothetically, because I am not yet sure of all the facts, but, if the facts turn out to be as they have reached us at present, it is quite clear that there is an obligation on this country to do its utmost to prevent the consequences to which those facts will lead if they are undisputed.

What other policy is there before the House? There is but one way in which the Government could make certain at the present moment of keeping outside this war, and that would be that it should immediately issue a proclamation of unconditional neutrality. We cannot do that; we have made the commitment to France that I have read to the House which prevents us doing that. We have got the consideration of Belgium which prevents us also from any unconditional neutrality, and, without these conditions absolutely satisfied and satisfactory, we are bound not to shrink from proceeding to the use of all the forces in our power. If we did take that line by saying, "We will have nothing whatever to do with this matter" under no conditions—the Belgian treaty obligations, the possible position in the Mediterranean, with damage to British interests, and what may happen to France from our failure to support France—if we were to say that all those things matter nothing, were as nothing, and to say we would stand aside, we should, I believe, sacrifice our respect and good name and reputation before the world, and should not escape the most serious and grave economic consequences. . . .

We Worked for Peace Beyond the Last Moment

My object has been to explain the view of the government, and to place before the House the issue and the choice. I do not for a moment conceal, after what I have said, and after the information, incomplete as it is, that I have given to the House with regard to Belgium, that we must be prepared, and we are prepared, for the consequences of having to use all the strength we have at any moment—we know not how soon—to defend ourselves and to take our part. We know, if the facts all be as I have stated them, though I have announced no intending aggressive action on our part, no final decision to resort to force at a moment's notice, until we know the whole of the case, that the use of it may be forced upon us. As far as the forces of the Crown are concerned, we are ready. I believe the Prime Minister [Herbert Henry Asquith] and my right honorable friend, the First Lord of the Admiralty [Sir Winston Churchill], have no doubt what ever that the readiness and the efficiency of those forces were never at a higher mark than they are to-day, and never was there a time when confidence was more justified in the power of the Navy to protect our commerce and to protect our shores. The thought is with us always of the suffering and misery entailed, from which no country in Europe will escape by abstention, and from which no neutrality will save us. The amount of harm that must be done by an enemy ship to our trade is infinitesimal, compared with the amount of harm that must be done by the economic condition that is caused on the Continent.

The most awful responsibility is resting upon the Government in deciding what to advise the House of Commons to do. We have disclosed our minds to the House of Commons. We have disclosed the issue, the information which we have, and made clear to the House, I trust, that we are prepared to face that situation, and that should it develop, as probably it may develop, we will face it. We worked for peace up to the last moment, and beyond the last moment. How hard, how persistently, and how earnestly we strove for peace last week the House will see from the papers that will be before it.

But that is over, as far as the peace of Europe is concerned. We are now face to face with a situation and all the consequences which it may yet have to unfold. We believe we shall have the support of the House at large in proceeding to whatever the consequences may be and whatever measures may be forced upon us by the development of facts or action taken by others. I believe the country, so quickly has the situation been forced upon it, has not had time to realize the issue. It perhaps is still thinking of the quarrel between Austria and Serbia, and not the complications of this matter which have grown out of the quarrel between Austria and Serbia. Russia and Germany we know are at war. We do not yet know officially that Austria, the ally whom Germany is to support, is yet at war with Russia. We know that a good deal has been happening on the French frontier. We do not know that the German Ambassador has left Paris.

The situation has developed so rapidly that technically, as regards the condition of the war, it is most difficult to describe what has actually happened. I wanted to bring out the underlying issues which would affect our own conduct and our own policy, and to put them clearly. I have now put the vital facts before the House, and if, as seems not improbable, we are forced, and rapidly forced, to take our stand upon those issues, then I believe, when the country realizes what is at stake, what the real issues are, the magnitude of the impending dangers in the west of Europe, which I have endeavored to describe to the House, we hall be supported through out, not only by the House of Commons, but by the determination, the resolution the courage, and the endurance of the whole country.

Germany's Reasons for War

Theobald von Bethmann Hollweg

Theobald von Bethmann Hollweg was appointed imperial chancellor of Germany, despite his inexperience in foreign affairs, serving from 1909 to 1917. On August 4, 1914, he gave the following speech before the Reichstag (German parliament). His address outlines the causes of war from the German point of view. According to von Bethmann Hollweg, Russia's mobilization against the Austro-Hungarian border and its subsequent refusal to withdraw led Germany to declare war on Russia. He says that German kaiser (king) Wilhelm II sought peace with Russia but that the Russian czar ignored such overtures. Von Bethmann Hollweg also states that France violated the peace through its use of border patrols, bombing, and French military incursions into German territory. He states that it is for these reasons that Germany must now prepare to fight. The nation must, the chancellor says, protect the territories it won from France in 1870.

By the time this speech was delivered on August 4, German troops had already entered the neutral nations of Luxembourg and Belgium. This violation of Belgian neutrality led to Great Britain's declaration of war on Germany that same day.

 tremendous crisis threatens Europe. Since we won for ourselves the German Empire and earned the respect of the world for forty-four years we have lived

Theobald von Bethmann Hollweg, speech before the Reichstag, August 4, 1914.

in peace and have protected the peace of Europe [this refers to the founding of the German Empire in 1871]. By peaceful labor we waxed strong and mighty and consequently aroused envy. With firm endurance we have seen how, under the pretext that Germany was eager for war, enmity was fostered in the East and West and chains were forged against us. The wind thus sown now rises in storm. We wished to live on in peaceful labor and from the Kaiser to the youngest soldier went the unexpressed vow: Only in defense of a just cause shall our sword fly from its scabbard. The day when we must draw it has come upon us against our will, against our honest efforts. Russia has set the torch to the house. We are forced to war against Russia and France.

Russia's Mobilization Prompted Germany's Reaction

Gentlemen, a series of documents put together in the stress of events which are crowding upon one another, has been placed before you. Allow me to bring out the facts which characterize our attitude.

From the first moment of the Austro-Serbian crisis we declared that this affair must be restricted to Austria-Hungary and Serbia and we worked to that end. All the cabinets, especially that of England, represent the same point of view. Russia alone declared that she must have a word in the settlement of this dispute. With this the danger of European entanglements raised its threatening head. As soon as the first definite reports of military preparations in Russia were received, we stated to St. Petersburg in a friendly but emphatic way that warlike measures against Austria would find us on the side of our ally and that military preparations against ourselves would compel us to take counter measures, but mobilization is very near war. Russia gave us solemn assurances of her desire for peace. And that she was making no military preparations against us. In the meantime England sought to mediate between St. Petersburg and Vienna, in which she was warmly supported by us. On July 28th the Kaiser [Wilhelm II, the ruler of Germany] besought the Czar [Nicholas II, the ruler of Russia] by telegram to bear in mind that it was the right and duty of Austria-Hungary to defend herself against the Pan-Serbian agitation, which threatened to undermine Austria-Hungary's existence. The Kaiser drew the attention of the Czar to the fact that the solidarity of monarchical interests was threatened by the crime of Sarajevo. He begged him to give his personal support in clearing away the differences. At about the same time, and before the receipt of this telegram, the Czar on his side begged the Kaiser for his help, and asked him to advise moderation in Vienna. The Kaiser undertook the rôle of mediator. But scarcely had the action ordered by him been started, when Russia mobilized all her forces directed against Austria-Hungary. Austria-Hungary, however, had only mobilized those army corps which were directly aimed at Serbia; only two army corps toward the North, far away from the Russian frontier.

The Kaiser immediately called the Czar's attention to the fact that by reason of this mobilization of the Russian forces against Austria, his rôle of mediator, undertaken at the Czar's request, was rendered more difficult if not impossible. Nevertheless, we continued our work of mediation in Vienna, going to the utmost bounds—permitted by our treaty relations. During this time Russia, of her own accord, renewed her assurances that she was not taking any military measures against us.

Germany Demands Russian Demobilization

July 31st [1914] arrived. In Vienna the decision was to be made. By our efforts up to that time we had succeeded in bringing it about that Vienna again took up the discussion with St. Petersburg through direct conversations which had ceased for some time. But even before the final decision had been reached in Vienna, came the news that Russia had mobilized her entire military force against us as well. The Russian government, which knew from our repeated representations what mobilization on our frontier meant, did not notify us of this mobilization, nor did it give us any explanation of it. Not before the afternoon of the 31st did a telegram come from the Czar to the Kaiser, in which he guaranteed that his army would take up no provocative attitude against us. But mobilization on our frontier had been in full progress since the night between July 30th and 31st. While we, at the request of Russia, were meditating in Vienna, the Russian forces drew up along our long and almost entirely open frontier; and France while not yet mobilizing nevertheless admits that she was taking military measures.

And we—up to that moment—we purposely had not called a single reserve, for the sake of European peace. Were we still to wait patiently until perhaps the powers between whom we are wedged chose the time to strike? To subject Germany to this danger would have been a crime! For that reason, still on the 31st we demanded Russian demobilization as the only measure which could still preserve the peace of Europe. The Imperial Ambassador in St. Petersburg was furthermore instructed to declare to the Russian Government that, in case of a rejection of our demand, we should have to consider that a state of war existed.

The Imperial Ambassador carried out these instructions. How Russia has replied to our demand for demobilization, we still do not know to-day. No telegraphic communications in regard to this have reached us although the telegraph has delivered many less important messages.

Thus, when the time limit expired, the Kaiser saw himself forced on August 1st, at 5 o'clock in the afternoon, to order the mobilization of our forces.

France Violated the Peace

At the same time we had to assure ourselves as to what France's position would be. To our definite question as to whether she would remain neutral in case of a German-Russian war, France replied that she would do as her interests demanded. This was an evasive reply to our question, if not a refusal.

The Kaiser nevertheless gave the order to respect the French frontier absolutely. This order was strictly carried out with a single exception. France, who mobilized at the same time that we did, declared that she would respect a zone of 10 kilometres from the frontier. And what actually occurred?

Aviators throwing bombs, cavalry patrols, French companies breaking into our territory! In this manner France, although no state of war had yet been declared, had violated the peace, and actually attacked us.

In regard to the one exception mentioned I have the following report from the Chief of the General Staff: "Of the French complaints in regard to the violation of the frontier from our side, we admit only one. Against express command, a patrol of the 14th Army Corps, apparently led by an officer, crossed the frontier on August 2nd. This patrol was apparently shot down—only one man has returned. But long before this single case of frontier infringement, French aviators penetrated into Southern Germany and threw bombs on our railways and at the 'Schlucht Pass' French troops have attacked our frontier patrols. Up to now our troops, according to order, have confined themselves entirely to defensive action" This is the report of the General Staff.

Gentlemen, we are now in a state of necessity, and necessity knows no law. Our troops have occupied Luxemburg; perhaps they have already entered Belgian territory. Gentlemen, this violates the rules of international law. The French government declared in Brussels that it was willing to respect the neutrality of Belgium as long as the enemy respected it. But we knew that France stood ready to invade. France could wait, we could not. A French attack on our flank on the lower Rhine might have been fatal to us. We were thus forced to ignore the just protests of the Luxemburg and Belgian governments. The wrong—I speak openly—the wrong that we do now, we will try to make good again, as soon as our military ends have been reached. Whoever is threatened as we are, and battles for all that is sacred, dares think only of how he can hack his way out!

Gentlemen, we stand shoulder to shoulder with Austria-Hungary.

The Great Hour of Trial for Germany

As to England's attitude, the declarations which Sir Edward Grey made yesterday in the House of Commons make clear the standpoint adopted by the English government. We have declared to the English government that, as long as England remains neutral our fleet will not attack the north coast of France and that we will not injure the territorial integrity and independence of Belgium. This declaration I now repeat before the whole world. And I may add that as long as England remains neutral we shall be ready, if equal assurances are given, to take no hostile measures against French merchant vessels.

Gentlemen, this is what has happened. I repeat the words of the Kaiser, "Germany enters the fight with a clear conscience!" We battle for the fruits of our peaceful labors, for the inheritance of a great past and for our future. The fifty years have not yet passed in which Moltke[1] said we should have to stand armed, ready to defend our inheritance, and the conquest of 1870. Now the great hour of trial has struck for our people. But we meet it with a clear confidence. Our army stands in the field, our fleet is ready for battle backed by the entire German people. The entire German people to the last man!

You, gentlemen, know the full extent of your duty. The bills before you need no further explanation. I beg you to pass them speedily.

---

1. Moltke the Elder was a Prussian general noted for important military victories against Austria (1866) and France (1870) that allowed for Germany to become a unified country.

Belgium Must Defend Its Territory

Albert I

King Albert I, ruler of Belgium from 1909 to 1934, was
aware that his country was the only wide-open space between the antagonistic nations of France and Germany.
As a result, King Albert's foreign policy strategy was to
refrain from alliances. Thus, Belgium maintained a policy
of neutrality and did not join either the Triple Alliance
(Germany, Austria-Hungary, and Italy) or the Triple Entente (Great Britain, France, and Russia). In July 1914
the Belgian army positioned itself along Belgium's borders
as a result of Germany's warlike statements following the
assassination of Austrian archduke Francis Ferdinand.
On August 2, 1914, Germany issued Belgium an ultimatum that stated that the nation must either fight or be
conquered. The Belgian minister of foreign affairs replied
that Belgium would resist any nation that violated its
neutrality. On August 4 a second ultimatum was sent to
Belgium stating that Germany would force a pass
through Belgian territory. The German army then invaded the country, thus violating Belgium's neutral
stance. On that same day, King Albert expressed his reaction to these events in the following address to the Belgian parliament. By the time he spoke, war was inevitable. As a means of resisting this threat to Belgium's
independence, the king urged his people to exhibit calm
courage and unity. He called upon the military to fulfill
its duty to defend the Belgian nation. He also asked the
civilian population to make the sacrifices that may be required for this endeavor. King Albert's words demon-

Albert I, address to the Belgian Parliament, August 4, 1914.

strate his confidence that Belgium will succeed and that
the nation's people will remain loyal to their king and to
their country.

Never since 1830 has a more grave moment come to
Belgium: the integrity of our territory is threatened.
The strength of our just cause, the sympathy
which Belgium, proud of her free institutions, and of her
moral conquests, has never ceased to enjoy at the hands of
other nations, the fact that our independent existence is necessary for the balance of power in Europe, these considerations give rise to hope that the events which we fear will not
take place.

But if our hopes fail, if we must resist the invasion of our
soil and must defend our threatened homes, this duty, hard
though it be, will find us ordered and prepared for the greatest sacrifices.

From this moment, with a view to meet every contin-
gency, the valiant youth of our nation stand ready, firmly resolved with the traditional tenacity and calmness of the Belgians to defend their fatherland at a moment of danger.

To them I send a brotherly greeting in the name of the nation. Throughout Flanders and the country of Wallonie in
town and country one sentiment alone fills every heart—patriotism; one vision alone fills every mind—our threatened
independence. One duty alone is laid upon our wills, stub-
born resistance.

At this grave moment two virtues are indispensable—
courage, calm but firm, and close union among all Belgians.

Striking evidence of both these virtues is already before
the eyes of a nation full of enthusiasm.

The faultless mobilization of our army, the multitude of
volunteers, the devotion of the civil population, the self-
sacrifice of families have shown incontestably that the whole
Belgian people is carried away by stimulating courage. The
moment has come.

I have called you together, gentlemen, to give to the Legislative Chambers an opportunity to associate themselves with

the impulses of the people in the same sentiment of sacrifice. Gentlemen, you will know how to deal urgently with all the measures which the situation requires for the war and for public order.

When I see this enthusiastic gathering in which there is only one party, that of the fatherland, in which at this moment all hearts beat as one, my mind goes back to the Congress of 1830, and I ask of you gentlemen, are you determined unswervingly to maintain intact the whole patrimony of our ancestors?

No one in the country will fail in his duty.

"A Country Which Defends Itself Commands the Respect of All"

The army, strong and disciplined, is fit to do this task: my Government and I have full confidence in its leader and its soldiers.

The Government, firmly attached to the populace and supported by them, is conscious of its responsibilities, and will bear them to the end with the deliberate conviction that the efforts of all united in the most fervent and generous patriotism will safeguard the supreme good of the country.

If the foreigner, disregarding the neutrality whose every duty we have always scrupulously observed, should violate our territory, he will find all Belgians grouped around their sovereign who will never betray his coronation oath, and around a Government possessing the absolute confidence of the entire nation.

I have faith in our destiny; a country which defends itself commands the respect of all; such a country shall never perish.

God will be with us in this just cause.

Long live independent Belgium.

France Will Have Right on Its Side

Raymond Poincaré

Raymond Poincaré was the president of France from 1913 to 1920. Upon taking office in January 1913, he expressed his belief that, because of increased German militarism over the last several decades, war in Europe was an eventuality. As a result, Poincaré strengthened French armed forces and further consolidated alliances with Britain and Russia. Shortly after the war began, he asked the French political parties to put aside their differences and form a "sacred union" (*l'union sacreé*) government for the duration of the conflict.

Poincaré made the following speech to the French parliament on August 5, 1914, two days after Germany's declaration of war on France. By that time, the German military had implemented the Schlieffen Plan, which was a strategy to send soldiers through neutral Belgium in order to attack France. Poincaré's address calls on the French troops to defend the honor of the country and reminds the soldiers that the nation is unanimous in its support for them. The president also tells the nation that France is on the side of righteousness and that with the help of Great Britain and Russia, France will prevail.

Gentlemen:

France has just been the object of a violent and premeditated attack, which is an insolent defiance of the law of nations. Before any declaration of war had been

Raymond Poincaré, address to the French Parliament, August 5, 1914.

sent to us, even before the German Ambassador had asked for his passports, our territory has been violated. The German Empire has waited till yesterday evening to give at this late stage the true name to a state of things which it had already created.

A Policy of Prudence, Wisdom, and Moderation

For more than forty years the French, in sincere love of peace, have buried at the bottom of their heart the desire for legitimate reparation.

They have given to the world the example of a great nation which, definitely raised from defeat by the exercise of will, patience, and labour, has only used its renewed and rejuvenated strength in the interest of progress and for the good of humanity.

Since the ultimatum of Austria opened a crisis which threatened the whole of Europe, France has persisted in following and in recommending on all sides a policy of prudence, wisdom, and moderation.

To her there can be imputed no act, no movement, no word, which has not been peaceful and conciliatory.

At the hour when the struggle is beginning, she has the right, in justice to herself, of solemnly declaring that she has made, up to the last moment, supreme efforts to avert the war now about to break out, the crushing responsibility for which the German Empire will have to bear before history. . . . Our fine and courageous army, which France today accompanies with her maternal thought has risen eager to defend the honour of the flag and the soil of the country.

The President of the Republic interpreting the unanimous feeling of the country, expresses to our troops by land and sea the admiration and confidence of every Frenchman.

Self-Control Is the Best Guarantee of Victory

Closely united in a common feeling, the nation will persevere with the cool self-restraint of which, since the beginning of the crisis, she has given daily proof. Now, as always, she will know how to harmonise the most noble daring and most ardent enthusiasm with that self-control which is the sign of enduring energy and is the best guarantee of victory.

In the war which is beginning, France will have Right on her side, the eternal power of which cannot with impunity be disregarded by nations any more than by individuals.

She will be heroically defended by all her sons; nothing will break their sacred union before the enemy; today they are joined together as brothers in a common indignation against the aggressor, and in a common patriotic faith.

She is faithfully helped by Russia, her ally; she is supported by the loyal friendship of Great Britain.

And already from every part of the civilised world sympathy and good wishes are coming to her. For today once again she stands before the universe for Liberty, Justice, and Reason.

'Haut les coeurs et vive la France! ["Lift your hearts and long live France!"]'.

Russia Enters the War with Confidence

Nicholas II

Russia was the first of the Triple Entente powers (Russia, France, and Great Britain) to engage in war with Germany. Following the Austrian archduke's assassination by a Serbian anarchist, Austria-Hungary sent an ultimatum to the Serbian government. One of the demands was that members of the Black Hand, the group to which assassin Gavrilo Princip belonged, be arrested and sent to Vienna for trial. Austria-Hungary, supported by its German ally, threatened to attack Serbia if the demands were not met. Serbia appealed to Russia for help, and on July 26, 1914, Russia promised to help Serbia if Austria-Hungary attacked. Two days later Austria-Hungary declared war on Serbia. Russian troops mobilized, and Germany declared war on Russia on August 1.

Czar Nicholas II, Russia's monarch and the last ruler of the Romanov dynasty, made this speech at the Winter Palace on August 8, 1914. In it, he announces the start of the war and appeals to the Russian people to support the war effort. He expresses confidence that the war will have a conclusion favorable for Russia. He mentions that Russian dignity and honor must be upheld. In addition, he notes that Russia is fighting to protect its fellow Slavic people.

Nicholas II, speech at the Winter Palace, August 8, 1914.

I greet you in these significant and troubled times which Russia is experiencing. Germany, and after her Austria, has declared war on Russia. Such an uplifting of patriotic feeling, love for our homes, and devotion to the Throne, which has swept over our land like a hurricane, serves in my eyes, and I think in yours, as a guarantee that our Great Mother Russia will by the help of our Lord God bring the war to a successful conclusion. In this united outburst of affection and readiness for all sacrifices, even that of life itself, I feel the possibility of upholding our strength, and quietly and with confidence look forward to the future.

We are not only protecting our honor and our dignity within the limits of our land, but also that of our brother Slavs, who are of one blood and faith with us. At this time I observe with joy that the feeling of unity among the Slavs has been brought into strong prominence throughout all Russia. I believe that you, each and all, in your place can sustain this Heaven-sent trial and that we all, beginning with myself, will fulfill our duty to the end. Great is the God of our Russian land!

CHAPTER
TWO

The United States Enters the War

"The World Must Be Made Safe for Democracy"

Woodrow Wilson

Woodrow Wilson was elected president of the United States in 1912 and again in 1916. When war broke out in Europe in August 1914, Wilson declared that the United States would maintain a neutral stance. Germany, meanwhile, engaged in unrestricted submarine warfare. American public opinion turned against Germany in May 1915 after the deliberate sinking of the passenger liner *Lusitania*, which was carrying American and British citizens. America remained neutral, but in January 1917, Germany resumed submarine warfare and the United States broke off its diplomatic relationship with Germany. That same month German foreign secretary Arthur Zimmermann sent a telegram, in code, to the German minister in Mexico City. According to this note, Germany promised to help Mexico regain U.S. territory if Mexico would aid the German cause. The British government intercepted the telegram and showed it to Wilson on February 24, 1917. The Zimmermann telegram was published in the American press on March 1.

These events of early 1917 set America on the course to war. In a special meeting of Congress on April 2, 1917, Wilson gave a lengthy speech about Germany's warfare and tactics of intrigue. In the speech Wilson argues that armed neutrality is no longer feasible and that the U.S. entry into the war is morally necessary. The key theme and a well-known phrase in this address is Wil-

---

Woodrow Wilson, address to the United States Congress, April 2, 1917.

son's insistence that America must enter the war in order to make the world safe for democracy. He says that the principles of peace and justice, threatened by imperial Germany, must be vindicated.

I have called the Congress into extraordinary session because there are serious, very serious, choices of policy to be made, and made immediately, which it was neither right nor constitutionally permissible that I should assume the responsibility of making.

Germany's Submarine Warfare

On the 3rd of February last [1917], I officially laid before you the extraordinary announcement of the Imperial German government that on and after the 1st day of February it was its purpose to put aside all restraints of law or of humanity and use its submarines to sink every vessel that sought to approach either the ports of Great Britain and Ireland or the western coasts of Europe or any of the ports controlled by the enemies of Germany within the Mediterranean.

That had seemed to be the object of the German submarine warfare earlier in the war, but since April of last year the Imperial [German] government had somewhat restrained the commanders of its undersea craft in conformity with its promise then given to us that passenger boats should not be sunk and that due warning would be given to all other vessels which its submarines might seek to destroy, when no resistance was offered or escape attempted, and care taken that their crews were given at least a fair chance to save their lives in their open boats. The precautions taken were meager and haphazard enough, as was proved in distressing instance after instance in the progress of the cruel and unmanly business, but a certain degree of restraint was observed.

The new policy [Germany's unrestricted submarine warfare policy] has swept every restriction aside. Vessels of every kind, whatever their flag, their character, their cargo, their destination, their errand, have been ruthlessly sent to the bottom without warning and without thought of help or mercy for those on board, the vessels of friendly neutrals along with those of belligerents. Even hospital ships and ships carrying relief to the sorely bereaved and stricken people of Belgium, though the latter were provided with safe conduct through the proscribed areas by the German government itself and were distinguished by unmistakable marks of identity, have been sunk with the same reckless lack of compassion or of principle.

I was for a little while unable to believe that such things would in fact be done by any government that had hitherto subscribed to the humane practices of civilized nations. International law had its origin in the attempt to set up some law which would be respected and observed upon the seas, where no nation had right of dominion and where lay the free highways of the world. By painful stage after stage has that law been built up, with meager enough results, indeed, after all was accomplished that could be accomplished, but always with a clear view, at least, of what the heart and conscience of mankind demanded.

This minimum of right the German government has swept aside under the plea of retaliation and necessity and because it had no weapons which it could use at sea except these which it is impossible to employ as it is employing them without throwing to the winds all scruples of humanity or of respect for the understandings that were supposed to underlie the intercourse of the world. I am not now thinking of the loss of property involved, immense and serious as that is, but only of the wanton and wholesale destruction of the lives of noncombatants, men, women, and children, engaged in pursuits which have always, even in the darkest periods of modern history, been deemed innocent and legitimate. Property can be paid for; the lives of peaceful and innocent people cannot be.

The Challenge to Mankind

The present German submarine warfare against commerce is a warfare against mankind. It is a war against all nations. American ships have been sunk, American lives taken in ways which it has stirred us very deeply to learn of; but the ships and people of other neutral and friendly nations have been sunk and overwhelmed in the waters in the same way. There has been no discrimination. The challenge is to all mankind.

Each nation must decide for itself how it will meet it. The choice we make for ourselves must be made with a moderation of counsel and a temperateness of judgment befitting our character and our motives as a nation. We must put excited feeling away. Our motive will not be revenge or the victorious assertion of the physical might of the nation, but only the vindication of right, of human right, of which we are only a single champion.

When I addressed the Congress on the 26th of February last [1917], I thought that it would suffice to assert our neutral rights with arms, our right to use the seas against unlawful interference, our right to keep our people safe against unlawful violence. But armed neutrality, it now appears, is impracticable. Because submarines are in effect outlaws when used as the German submarines have been used against merchant shipping, it is impossible to defend ships against their attacks as the law of nations has assumed that merchantmen would defend themselves against privateers or cruisers, visible craft giving chase upon the open sea.

It is common prudence in such circumstances, grim necessity indeed, to endeavor to destroy them before they have shown their own intention. They must be dealt with upon sight, if dealt with at all. The German government denies the right of neutrals to use arms at all within the areas of the sea which it has proscribed, even in the defense of rights which no modern publicist has ever before questioned their right to defend. The intimation is conveyed that the armed guards which we have placed on our merchant ships will be treated as beyond the pale of law and subject to be dealt with as pirates would be.

Armed neutrality is ineffectual enough at best; in such circumstances and in the face of such pretensions it is worse than ineffectual: it is likely only to produce what it was meant to prevent; it is practically certain to draw us into the war without either the rights or the effectiveness of belligerents. There is one choice we cannot make, we are incapable of making: we will not choose the path of submission and suffer the most sacred rights of our nation and our people to be ignored or violated. The wrongs against which we now array ourselves are no common wrongs; they cut to the very roots of human life.

Nothing Less than War

With a profound sense of the solemn and even tragical character of the step I am taking and of the grave responsibilities which it involves, but in unhesitating obedience to what I deem my constitutional duty, I advise that the Congress declare the recent course of the Imperial German government to be in fact nothing less than war against the government and people of the United States; that it formally accept the status of belligerent which has thus been thrust upon it; and that it take immediate steps, not only to put the country in a more thorough state of defense but also to exert all its power and employ all its resources to bring the government of the German Empire to terms and end the war.

What this will involve is clear. It will involve the utmost practicable cooperation in counsel and action with the governments now at war with Germany and, as incident to that, the extension to those governments of the most liberal financial credits, in order that our resources may so far as possible be added to theirs. It will involve the organization and mobilization of all the material resources of the country to supply the materials of war and serve the incidental needs of the nation in the most abundant and yet the most economical and efficient way possible. It will involve the immediate full equipment of the Navy in all respects but particularly in supplying it with the best means of dealing with the enemy's submarines. It will involve the immediate addition to the armed forces of the United States already provided for by law in case of war at least 500,000 men, who should, in my opinion, be chosen upon the principle of universal liability to service, and also the authorization of subsequent additional increments of equal force so soon as they may be needed and can be handled in training.

It will involve also, of course, the granting of adequate credits to the government, sustained, I hope, so far as they can equitably be sustained by the present generation, by well-conceived taxation. I say sustained so far as may be equitable by taxation because it seems to me that it would be most unwise to base the credits which will now be necessary entirely on money borrowed. It is our duty, I most respectfully urge, to protect our people so far as we may against the very serious hardships and evils which would be likely to arise out of the inflation which would be produced by vast loans.

In carrying out the measures by which these things are to be accomplished, we should keep constantly in mind the wisdom of interfering as little as possible in our own preparation and in the equipment of our own military forces with the duty—for it will be a very practical duty—of supplying the nations already at war with Germany with the materials which they can obtain only from us or by our assistance. They are in the field and we should help them in every way to be effective there.

I shall take the liberty of suggesting, through the several executive departments of the government, for the consideration of your committees, measures for the accomplishment of the several objects I have mentioned. I hope that it will be your pleasure to deal with them as having been framed after very careful thought by the branch of the government upon which the responsibility of conducting the war and safeguarding the nation will most directly fall.

While we do these things, these deeply momentous things, let us be very clear, and make very clear to all the world, what our motives and our objects are. My own thought has not been driven from its habitual and normal course by the unhappy events of the last two months, and I do not believe that the thought of the nation has been altered or clouded by them. . . .

Our object now, as then, is to vindicate the principles of peace and justice in the life of the world as against selfish and autocratic power and to set up among the really free and self-governed peoples of the world such a concert of purpose and of action as will henceforth ensure the observance of those principles. Neutrality is no longer feasible or desirable where the peace of the world is involved and the freedom of its peoples, and the menace to that peace and freedom lies in the existence of autocratic governments backed by organized force which is controlled wholly by their will, not by the will of their people. We have seen the last of neutrality in such circumstances. We are at the beginning of an age in which it will be insisted that the same standards of conduct and of responsibility for wrong done shall be observed among nations and their governments that are observed among the individual citizens of civilized states.

The German Government Is the Problem

We have no quarrel with the German people. We have no feeling toward them but one of sympathy and friendship. It was not upon their impulse that their government acted in entering this war. It was not with their previous knowledge or approval. It was a war determined upon as wars used to be determined upon in the old, unhappy days when peoples were nowhere consulted by their rulers and wars were provoked and waged in the interest of dynasties or of little groups of ambitious men who were accustomed to use their fellowmen as pawns and tools.

Self-governed nations do not fill their neighbor states with spies or set the course of intrigue to bring about some critical posture of affairs which will give them an opportunity to strike and make conquest. Such designs can be successfully worked out only under cover and where no one has the right to ask questions. Cunningly contrived plans of deception or aggression, carried, it may be, from generation to generation, can be worked out and kept from the light only within the privacy of courts or behind the carefully guarded confidences of a narrow and privileged class. They are happily impossible where public opinion commands and insists upon full information concerning all the nation's affairs.

A steadfast concert for peace can never be maintained except by a partnership of democratic nations. No autocratic government could be trusted to keep faith within it or observe its covenants. It must be a league of honor, a partnership of opinion. Intrigue would eat its vitals away; the plottings of inner circles who could plan what they would and render account to no one would be a corruption seated at its very heart. Only free peoples can hold their purpose and their honor steady to a common end and prefer the interests of mankind to any narrow interest of their own.

Does not every American feel that assurance has been added to our hope for the future peace of the world by the wonderful and heartening things that have been happening within the last few weeks in Russia? Russia was known by those who knew it best to have been always in fact democratic at heart, in all the vital habits of her thought, in all the intimate relationships of her people that spoke their natural instinct, their habitual attitude toward life. The autocracy that crowned the summit of her political structure, long as it had stood and terrible as was the reality of its power, was not in fact Russian in origin, character, or purpose; and now it has been shaken off and the great, generous Russian people have been added in all their naive majesty and might to the forces that are fighting for freedom in the world, for justice, and for peace. Here is a fit partner for a League of Honor.

One of the things that has served to convince us that the Prussian autocracy was not and could never be our friend is that from the very outset of the present war it has filled our unsuspecting communities and even our offices of government with spies and set criminal intrigues everywhere afoot against our national unity of counsel, our peace within and without, our industries and our commerce. Indeed, it is now evident that its spies were here even before the war began; and it is unhappily not a matter of conjecture but a fact proved in our courts of justice that the intrigues which have more than once come perilously near to disturbing the peace and dislocating the industries of the country have been carried on at the instigation, with the support, and even under the personal direction of official agents of the Imperial government accredited to the government of the United States.

Even in checking these things and trying to extirpate them, we have sought to put the most generous interpretation possible upon them because we knew that their source lay, not in any hostile feeling or purpose of the German people toward us (who were no doubt as ignorant of them as we ourselves were) but only in the selfish designs of a government that did what it pleased and told its people nothing. But they have played their part in serving to convince us at last that that government entertains no real friendship for us and means to act against our peace and security at its convenience. That it means to stir up enemies against us at our very doors the interceded note [the Zimmermann telegram] to the German minister at Mexico City is eloquent evidence.

We are accepting this challenge of hostile purpose because we know that in such a government, following such methods, we can never have a friend; and that in the presence of its organized power, always lying in wait to accomplish we know not what purpose, there can be no assured security for the democratic governments of the world. We are now about to accept gage of battle with this natural foe to liberty and shall, if necessary, spend the whole force of the nation to check and nullify its pretensions and its power. We are glad, now that we see the facts with no veil of false pretense about them, to fight thus for the ultimate peace of the world and for the liberation of its peoples, the German peoples included: for the rights of nations great and small and the privilege of men everywhere to choose their way of life and of obedience.

"The World Must Be Made Safe for Democracy"

The world must be made safe for democracy. Its peace must be planted upon the tested foundations of political liberty. We have no selfish ends to serve. We desire no conquest, no dominion. We seek no indemnities for ourselves, no material compensation for the sacrifices we shall freely make. We are but one of the champions of the rights of mankind. We shall be satisfied when those rights have been made as secure as the faith and the freedom of nations can make them.

Just because we fight without rancor and without selfish object, seeking nothing for ourselves but what we shall wish to share with all free peoples, we shall, I feel confident, conduct our operations as belligerents without passion and ourselves observe with proud punctilio the principles of right and of fair play we profess to be fighting for.

I have said nothing of the governments allied with the Imperial government of Germany because they have not made war upon us or challenged us to defend our right and our honor. The Austro-Hungarian government has, indeed, avowed its unqualified endorsement and acceptance of the reckless and lawless submarine warfare adopted now without disguise by the Imperial German government, and it has therefore not been possible for this government to receive Count Tarnowski, the ambassador recently accredited to this government by the Imperial and Royal government of Austria-Hungary; but that government has not actually engaged in warfare against citizens of the United States on the seas, and I take the liberty, for the present at least, of postponing a discussion of our relations with the authorities at Vienna. We enter this war only where we are clearly forced into it because there are no other means of defending our rights.

It will be all the easier for us to conduct ourselves as belligerents in a high spirit of right and fairness because we act without animus, not in enmity toward a people or with the desire to bring any injury or disadvantage upon them, but only in armed opposition to an irresponsible government which has thrown aside all considerations of humanity and of right and is running amuck. We are, let me say again, the sincere friends of the German people, and shall desire nothing so much as the early reestablishment of intimate relations of mutual advantage between us—however hard it may be for them, for the time being, to believe that this is spoken from our hearts.

We have borne with their present government through all these bitter months because of that friendship—exercising a patience and forbearance which would otherwise have been impossible. We shall, happily, still have an opportunity to prove that friendship in our daily attitude and actions toward the millions of men and women of German birth and native sympathy who live among us and share our life, and we shall be proud to prove it toward all who are in fact loyal to their neighbors and to the government in the hour of test. They are, most of them, as true and loyal Americans as if they had never known any, other fealty or allegiance. They will be prompt to stand with us in rebuking and restraining the few who may be of a different mind and purpose. If there should be disloyalty, it will be dealt with with a firm hand of stern repression; but, if it lifts its head at all, it will lift it only here and there and without countenance except from a lawless and malignant few.

It is a distressing and oppressive duty, gentlemen of the Congress, which I have performed in thus addressing you. There are, it may be, many months of fiery trial and sacrifice ahead of us. It is a fearful, thing to lead this great peaceful people into war, into the most terrible and disastrous of all wars, civilization itself seeming to be in, the balance. But the right is more precious than peace, and we shall fight for the things which we have always carried nearest our hearts—for democracy, for the right of those who submit to authority to have a voice in their own governments, for the rights and liberties of small nations, for a universal dominion of right by such a concert of free peoples as shall bring peace and safety to all nations and make the world itself at last free.

To such a task we can dedicate our lives and our fortunes, everything that we are and everything that we have, with the pride of those who know that the day has come when America is privileged to spend her blood and her might for the principles that gave her birth and happiness and the peace which she has treasured. God helping her, she can do no other.

An Unholy and Unrighteous War

George W. Norris

George W. Norris was a Republican from Nebraska who served thirty years in the U.S. Senate. He was a vocal opponent of President Woodrow Wilson's foreign policy before and after World War I. He felt that by entering the war, Americans would be fighting for profits, not principles. Norris gave this speech on April 4, 1917, while the resolution for Wilson's proposed war declaration was before the Senate. Norris states here that he is bitterly opposed to the United States entering the European war because the reasons for it are economically driven and prompted by the interests of Wall Street. As evidence, he cites a letter from a stockbroker to his customers that highlights the financial benefit of the United States entering the war. Norris argues that although industrialists will profit from the war, those men sacrificed in the fighting will not share in the prosperity. Thus, for Norris, the U.S. entry into war is unjustifiable.

While I am most emphatically and sincerely opposed to taking any step that will force our country into the useless and senseless war now being waged in Europe, yet, if this resolution passes, I shall not permit my feeling of opposition to its passage to interfere in any way with my duty either as a senator or as a citizen in bringing success and victory to American arms. I am bitterly opposed to my country entering the war, but if, notwithstanding my

George W. Norris, address to the United States Congress, April 4, 1917.

opposition, we do enter it, all of my energy and all of my power will be behind our flag in carrying it on to victory.

The resolution now before the Senate is a declaration of war. Before taking this momentous step, and while standing on the brink of this terrible vortex, we ought to pause and calmly and judiciously consider the terrible consequences of the step we are about to take. We ought to consider likewise the route we have recently traveled and ascertain whether we have reached our present position in a way that is compatible with the neutral position which we claimed to occupy at the beginning and through the various stages of this unholy and unrighteous war.

Rights and Duties

No close student of recent history will deny that both Great Britain and Germany have, on numerous occasions since the beginning of the war, flagrantly violated in the most serious manner the rights of neutral vessels and neutral nations under existing international law, as recognized up to the beginning of this war by the civilized world.

The reason given by the President [Woodrow Wilson] in asking Congress to declare war against Germany is that the German government has declared certain war zones, within which, by the use of submarines, she sinks, without notice, American ships and destroys American lives. . . . The first war zone was declared by Great Britain. She gave us and the world notice of it on the 4th day of November 1914. The zone became effective Nov. 5, 1914. . . . This zone so declared by Great Britain covered the whole of the North Sea. . . . The first German war zone was declared on the 4th day of February 1915, just three months after the British war zone was declared. Germany gave fifteen days' notice of the establishment of her zone, which became effective on the 18th day of February 1915. The German war zone covered the English Channel and the high seawaters around the British Isles. . . .

It is unnecessary to cite authority to show that both of these orders declaring military zones were illegal and contrary to international law. It is sufficient to say that our government has officially declared both of them to be illegal and has officially protested against both of them. The only difference is that in the case of Germany we have persisted in our protest, while in the case of England we have submitted.

What was our duty as a government and what were our rights when we were confronted with these extraordinary orders declaring these military zones? First, we could have defied both of them and could have gone to war against both of these nations for this violation of international law and interference with our neutral rights. Second, we had the technical right to defy one and to acquiesce in the other. Third, we could, while denouncing them both as illegal, have acquiesced in them both and thus remained neutral with both sides, although not agreeing with either as to the righteousness of their respective orders. We could have said to American shipowners that, while these orders are both contrary to international law and are both unjust, we do not believe that the provocation is sufficient to cause us to go to war for the defense of our rights as a neutral nation, and, therefore, American ships and American citizens will go into these zones at their own peril and risk.

Fourth, we might have declared an embargo against the shipping from American ports of any merchandise to either one of these governments that persisted in maintaining its military zone. We might have refused to permit the sailing of any ship from any American port to either of these military zones. In my judgment, if we had pursued this course, the zones would have been of short duration. England would have been compelled to take her mines out of the North Sea in order to get any supplies from our country. When her mines were taken out of the North Sea then the German ports upon the North Sea would have been accessible to American shipping and Germany would have been compelled to cease her submarine warfare in order to get any supplies from our nation into German North Sea ports.

There are a great many American citizens who feel that we owe it as a duty to humanity to take part in this war. Many instances of cruelty and inhumanity can be found on both sides. Men are often biased in their judgment on account of their sympathy and their interests. To my mind, what we ought to have maintained from the beginning was the strictest neutrality. If we had done this, I do not believe we would have been on the verge of war at the present time. We had a right as a nation, if we desired, to cease at any time to be neutral. We had a technical right to respect the English war zone and to disregard the German war zone, but we could not do that and be neutral.

Misled Patriotism

I have no quarrel to find with the man who does not desire our country to remain neutral. While many such people are moved by selfish motives and hopes of gain, I have no doubt but that in a great many instances, through what I believe to be a misunderstanding of the real condition, there are many honest, patriotic citizens who think we ought to engage in this war and who are behind the President in his demand that we should declare war against Germany. I think such people err in judgment and to a great extent have been misled as to the real history and the true facts by the almost unanimous demand of the great combination of wealth that has a direct financial interest in our participation in the war.

We have loaned many hundreds of millions of dollars to the Allies in this controversy. While such action was legal and countenanced by international law, there is no doubt in my mind but the enormous amount of money loaned to the Allies in this country has been instrumental in bringing about a public sentiment in favor of our country taking a course that would make every bond worth a hundred cents on the dollar and making the payment of every debt certain and sure. Through this instrumentality and also through the instrumentality of others who have not only made millions out of the war in the manufacture of munitions, etc., and who would expect to make millions more if our country can be drawn into the catastrophe, a large number of the great newspapers and news agencies of the country have been controlled and enlisted in the greatest propaganda that the world has ever known to manufacture sentiment in favor of war.

It is now demanded that the American citizens shall be used as insurance policies to guarantee the safe delivery of munitions of war to belligerent nations. The enormous profits of munition manufacturers, stockbrokers, and bond dealers must be still further increased by our entrance into the war. This has brought us to the present moment, when Congress, urged by the President and backed by the artificial sentiment, is about to declare war and engulf our country in the greatest holocaust that the world has ever known.

The Stockbroker's Position

In showing the position of the bondholder and the stockbroker, I desire to read an extract from a letter written by a member of the New York Stock Exchange to his customers. This writer says:

> Regarding the war as inevitable, Wall Street believes that it would be preferable to this uncertainty about the actual date of its commencement. Canada and Japan are at war and are more prosperous than ever before. The popular view is that stocks would have a quick, clear, sharp reaction immediately upon outbreak of hostilities, and that then they would enjoy an old-fashioned bull market such as followed the outbreak of war with Spain in 1898. The advent of peace would force a readjustment of commodity prices and would probably mean a postponement of new enterprises. As peace negotiations would be long drawn out, the period of waiting and uncertainty for business would be long. If the United States does not go to war, it is nevertheless good opinion that the preparedness program will compensate in good measure for the loss of the stimulus of actual war.

Here we have the Wall Street view. Here we have the man representing the class of people who will be made prosperous should we become entangled in the present war, who have already made millions of dollars, and who will make many hundreds of millions more if we get into the war. Here we have the cold-blooded proposition that war brings prosperity to that class of people who are within the viewpoint of this writer.

He expresses the view, undoubtedly, of Wall Street, and

of thousands of men elsewhere who see only dollars coming to them through the handling of stocks and bonds that will be necessary in case of war. "Canada and Japan" he says, "are at war, and are more prosperous than ever before."

Prosperity for Whom?

To whom does war bring prosperity? Not to the soldier who for the munificent compensation of $16 per month shoulders his musket and goes into the trench, there to shed his blood and to die if necessary; not to the brokenhearted widow who waits for the return of the mangled body of her husband; not to the mother who weeps at the death of her brave boy; not to the little children who shiver with cold; not to the babe who suffers from hunger; nor to the millions of mothers and daughters who carry broken hearts to their graves. War brings no prosperity to the great mass of common and patriotic citizens. It increases the cost of living of those who toil and those who already must strain every effort to keep soul and body together. War brings prosperity to the stock gambler on Wall Street—to those who are already in possession of more wealth than can be realized or enjoyed.

Again this writer says that if we cannot get war, "it is nevertheless good opinion that the preparedness program will compensate in good measure for the loss of the stimulus of actual war." That is, if we cannot get war, let us go as far in that direction as possible. If we cannot get war, let us cry for additional ships, additional guns, additional munitions, and everything else that will have a tendency to bring us as near as possible to the verge of war. And if war comes, do such men as these shoulder the musket and go into the trenches?

Their object in having war and in preparing for war is to make money. Human suffering and the sacrifice of human life are necessary, but Wall Street considers only the dollars and the cents. The men who do the fighting, the people who make the sacrifices are the ones who will not be counted in the measure of this great prosperity that he depicts. The stockbrokers would not, of course, go to war because the very object they have in bringing on the war is profit, and therefore they must remain in their Wall Street offices in order to share in that great prosperity which they say war will bring. The volunteer officer, even the drafting officer, will not find them. They will be concealed in their palatial offices on Wall Street, sitting behind mahogany desks, covered up with clipped coupons—coupons soiled with the sweat of honest toil, coupons stained with mothers' tears, coupons dyed in the lifeblood of their fellowmen.

We are taking a step today that is fraught with untold danger. We are going into war upon the command of gold. We are going to run the risk of sacrificing millions of our countrymen's lives in order that other countrymen may coin their lifeblood into money. And even if we do not cross the Atlantic and go into the trenches, we are going to pile up a debt that the tolling masses that shall come many generations after us will have to pay. Unborn millions will bend their backs in toil in order to pay for the terrible step we are now about to take.

We are about to do the bidding of wealth's terrible mandate. By our act we will make millions of our countrymen suffer, and the consequences of it may well be that millions of our brethren must shed their lifeblood, millions of broken-hearted women must weep, millions of children must suffer with cold, and millions of babes must die from hunger, and all because we want to preserve the commercial right of American citizens to deliver munitions of war to belligerent nations.

England Salutes American Comrades in Arms

David Lloyd George

In February 1917 the German high command adopted a policy of unrestricted submarine warfare. This policy was one of the factors that prompted the United States to declare war on Germany on April 6. At a meeting of the American Luncheon Club on April 12, British prime minister David Lloyd George delivered the following speech. In it, he extends his gratitude to the United States for having entered the war as an associate power on the side of the Allies. Lloyd George states that America's entry into the war reflects the Allied struggle for democracy and freedom in opposition to the military autocracy represented by Germany. He notes that Germany provoked the United States into war, and that American support will ensure an Allied victory and a beneficent peace. Lloyd George served as Great Britain's prime minister from 1916 until 1922.

I was invited to attend a small family luncheon—but when I entered this room I found that was another American legend—dispelled when I saw this great and impressive gathering. I am in the happy position, I think, of being the first British Minister of the Crown who, speaking on behalf of the people of this country, can salute the American nation as comrades in arms. I am glad. I am proud. I am glad not

David Lloyd George, address to the American Luncheon Club, Washington, DC, April 12, 1917.

merely because of the stupendous resources which this great nation can bring to the succor of the Alliance, but I rejoice as a Democrat[1] that the advent of the United States into this war gives the final stamp and seal to the character of the conflict as a struggle against military autocracy throughout the world.

U.S. Entry Represents a Fight for Human Liberty

That was the note that rang through the great deliverance of President Wilson. . . . The United States of America have a noble tradition, never broken, of having never engaged in a war except for liberty and this is the greatest struggle for liberty they have ever embarked upon. I am not at all surprised, when one recollects the wars of the past, that America took its time to make up its mind about the character of this struggle. In Europe most of the great wars of the past were waged for dynastic aggrandizements and for conquest. No wonder that when this great war started there were some elements of suspicion still lurking in the minds of the people of the United States of America. There were many who thought, perhaps, that kings were at their old tricks, and although they saw the gallant Republic of France, fighting, they, some of them perhaps, regarded France as the poor victim of conspiracy and of monarchical swashbucklers.

The fact that the United States of America has made up its mind finally makes it abundantly clear to the world that this is no struggle of that character, but a great fight for human liberty. They naturally did not know at first what we had endured in Europe for years from this military caste in Prussia.[2] It never reached as far as the United States of America. Prussia is not a democracy, but the Kaiser [Wilhelm II] promises it will be a democracy after the war. I think he is right. But Prussia not merely was not a democracy; Prussia was not a state. Prussia was an army. It had great industries, highly developed. It had a great educational system. It had its universities. It developed its sciences. But all these were subordinate to the one

1. This refers to upholding principles of democracy, not a party affiliation   2. A part of Germany, it was home to the monarchy. It is often used to mean Germany.

great predominant purpose of an all-conquering army which was to intimidate the world. The army was the spear-point of Prussia; the rest was merely the gilded shaft.

Prussian Tyranny Made Europe Uneasy

That is what we had to deal with in these old countries. It got on the nerves of Europe. They knew what it all meant. The Prussian army in recent times had waged three wars—all for conquest. And the incessant tramping of its legions through the streets of Prussia and on the parade grounds of Prussia had got into the Prussian head. The Kaiser, when he witnessed it on a grand scale in his reviews, got drunk with the sound of it. He delivered the law to the world, as though Potsdam were a new Sinai and he were uttering the law from the thunder-cloud. But make no mistake; Europe was uneasy. Europe was half intimidated; Europe was anxious; Europe was apprehensive. We knew the whole time what it meant. What we did not know was the moment it would come. This is the menace, this is the oppression, from which Europe has suffered for fifty years. It paralyzed the beneficent activities of all States, which ought to have been devoted to, and concentrated upon, the well-being of their people. They had to think about this menace, which was there constantly as a cloud, ready to burst over the land.

Take France. No one can tell except the Frenchman what they endured from this tyranny, patiently, gallantly, with dignity, until the hour of deliverance came. The best energies in democratic France have been devoted to defense against the impending terror. France was like a nation which has put up its right arm to ward off a blow, and it could not use the whole of its strength for the great things France was capable of. That great, bold, imaginative, fertile mind, which would otherwise have been cleaving new paths of progress, was paralyzed. This was the state of things we had to encounter.

This Is a Struggle for Freedom

The most characteristic of all Prussian institutions is the Hindenburg line. What is the Hindenburg line? The Hindenburg line is a line drawn in the territories of other people with a warning that the inhabitants of those territories shall not cross it at the peril of their lives. That line has been drawn in Europe for fifty years in many lands. . . .

Europe, after enduring this for generations, made up its mind at last that the Hindenburg line must be drawn along the legitimate frontiers of Germany herself. . . . It has been an undoubted fight for the emancipation of Europe and the emancipation of the world. It was hard at first for the people of America quite to appreciate that. Germany had not interfered to the same extent with their freedom, if at all. But at last she has endured the same experience to which Europe has been subjected. Americans were told they were not to be allowed to cross and recross the Atlantic except at their peril. American ships were sunk without warning. American subjects were drowned with hardly an apology, in fact as a matter of German right. At first America could hardly believe it. They could not think it possible that any sane people could behave in that manner. And they tolerated it once, they tolerated it twice, until at last it became clear that the Germans really meant it. Then America acted and acted promptly. The Hindenburg line was drawn along the shores of America and Americans were told they must not cross it. America said, "What is this?" and was told that this was a line beyond which they must not go. Then America said, "The place for that line is not the Atlantic, but on the Rhine, and we mean to help you roll it up." And they have started.

There are two great facts which clinch the argument that this is a great struggle for freedom. The first is the fact that America has come in. She could not have done otherwise. The second is the Russian Revolution.[3] When France in the eighteenth century sent her soldiers to America to fight for the freedom and independence of that land France also was an autocracy. But when the Frenchmen were in America their aim was freedom. They acquired a taste for freedom and they took it home, and France became free. That is the story of Russia. Russia engaged in this great war for the freedom of Serbia, of Montenegro, and Bulgaria. Russians have fought

3. In February/March 1917, the Russian Revolution ended the rule of the czar and the Romanov dynasty.

for the freedom of Europe, and they wanted to make their own country free. They have done it. The Russian Revolution is not merely the outcome of the struggle for freedom. It is a proof of its character as a struggle for liberty. And if the Russian people realize, as there is evidence they are doing, that national discipline is not incompatible with national freedom, and know that national discipline is essential to the security of national freedom, they will indeed become free people.

Germany Provoked America into War

I have been asking myself the question why is it that Germany deliberately in the third year of the war provoked America to this declaration, and to this action? Deliberately! Yes; resolutely! It has been suggested that the reason was that there were certain elements in American life which Germany was under the impression would make it impossible for the United States to declare war. That I can hardly believe; but the answer has been afforded by General Hindenburg himself in the very remarkable interview which appears, I think, this morning in the Press. He depended clearly on one of two things—that the submarine campaign would have destroyed international shipping to such an extent that England would have been put out of business before America was ready. According to his computation, America would not be ready for twelve months. He does not know America. Then alternatively, and when America was ready at the end of twelve months with her army, she would have no ships to transport that army to the field of battle. In Hindenburg's words, "America carries no weight." I suppose he means that she has no ships to carry on. That is undoubtedly their reckoning.

Well, it is not wise always to assume, even when the German General Staff has miscalculated, that they have had no ground for their calculation; and therefore it behooves the whole of the Allies—Britain and America in particular—to see that that reckoning of Von Hindenburg is as false as the one he made about the famous line which we have broken already. The road to victory, the guarantee of victory, the absolute assurance of victory, is to be found in one word—ships. In the second word—ships; in a third word—ships. I see that America, with that quickness of comprehension which characterizes your nation, fully realizes that, and to-day I observe that they have already made an arrangement to build—is it 1000?—3000-tonners for the Atlantic. I think that the German military advisers must already begin to realize that this is another of the tragic miscalculations which is going to lead them to disaster and to ruin.

America Will Wage a Successful War and Ensure Peace

But, Mr. Chairman, you will pardon me for just emphasizing that we are a slow people in these islands. Yes, but sure! Slowly, blunderingly; but we get there. You get there sooner, and that is why I am glad to see you in. But may I say we have been in this business for three years? We have made blunders; we generally do; we have tried every blunder. In golfing phraseology, we have gone through every bunker; but we have a good niblick stroke—and we are now right out on the course. May I respectfully suggest that it is worth America's while to study our blunders so as to begin just where we are now—not where we were three years ago? In war, time is everything, time has a tragic significance. A step taken to-day may lead to assured victory, but taken to-morrow may barely avert disaster. All the Allies have discovered that. It was a new country for us all. It was trackless, mapless; we had to go by instinct, but we found the way, and I am so glad that you are sending your great naval and military experts here just to exchange experiences with men who have been through all the dreary, anxious course of the last three years.

America has helped us even to win the battle of Arras[4]— this great battle. Those guns which destroyed the German trenches and shattered the barbed wire—I remember with some friends of mine I see here discussing the matter and arranging to order from America the machines to make those guns. Not all. You got your share; it was only a share, but it is a glorious one. America has been making guns, making

4. Also called the Battle of Vimy Ridge, this Allied offensive began April 19, 1917. It was the most successful western front advance by the Allies to date.

munitions, making machinery to prepare both, supplying us with steel, and she has got all that organization, that wonderful facility, adaptability, and resourcefulness of the great people who inhabit that great continent. Ah! it was a bad day for military autocracy in Prussia when she challenged the great Republic of the West. We know what America can do; and we also know that now she is in it she will do it. She will wage an effective and successful war.

There is something more important. She will ensure a beneficent peace. I am the last man in the world—knowing for three years what our difficulties have been, what our anxieties have been, what our fears have been—to deny that the succor which is given us from America is something to rejoice in, and rejoice greatly in; but I do not mind telling you that I rejoice even more in the knowledge that America is going to win her right to be at the conference table when the terms of peace are being discussed. That conference will settle the destiny of nations, the course of human life, for God knows how many ages. It would have been a tragedy for mankind if America had not been there, and there with all the influence, and the power, and the right, which she has now won by flinging herself into this great struggle.

I can see peace coming now, not a peace which would be a beginning of war, not a peace which would be an endless preparation for strife and bloodshed; but a real peace. The world is an old world which has never had peace. It has been rocking, swaying like the ocean, and Europe—poor Europe—has always lived under the menace of the sword. When this war began two-thirds of Europe was under autocratic rule. It is the other way about now, and democracy means peace. The democracy of France did not want war. The democracy of Italy hesitated long before entering the war.[5] The democracy of this country shrank from it and shuddered, and would never have entered that cauldron if it had not been for the invasion of Belgium. Democracy sought peace, strove for peace, and if Prussia had been a democracy there would have been no war.

---

5. Italy, though allied to Germany and Austria-Hungary prior to the war, declared neutrality in 1914. On May 23, 1915, Italy joined the war on the side of the Allies.

Attacking with the Dawn

But strange things have happened in this war, and stranger things are to come—and they are coming rapidly. There are times in history when the world spins so leisurely along its destined course that it seems for centuries to be at a standstill. There are also times when it rushes along at a giddy pace covering the track of centuries in a year. These are the times we are living in now. Six weeks ago Russia was an autocracy. She is now one of the most advanced democracies in the world. To-day we are waging the most devastating war that the world has ever seen. To-morrow—not perhaps a distant to-morrow—war may be abolished forever from the categories of human crimes. This may be something like that fierce outburst of winter which we are now witnessing before the complete triumph of spring.

It was written of those gallant men who won that victory on Monday [at the Battle of Arras]—men from Canada, from Australia, and from this old country—which has proved that in spite of its age it is not decrepit—it was written of those gallant men that they attacked with the dawn. Fitting work for the dawn to drive out of forty miles of French soil those miscreants who had defiled it for nearly three years. They attacked with the dawn. It is a significant phrase. The breaking up of the dark rule of the Turk, which for centuries has clouded the sunniest lands in the world, the freeing of Russia from the oppression which has covered it like a cloud for so long, the great declaration of President Wilson coming with the might of the great nation he represents in the struggle for liberty, are heralds of dawn. "They attacked with the dawn," and those men are marching forward in the full radiance of that dawn, and soon Frenchmen and Americans, British, Italians, and Russians, yea, Serbians, Belgians, Montenegrins, and Roumanians will march into the full light of perfect day.

"We Don't Believe in Conscription"

Emma Goldman

Emma Goldman, an anarchist and Russian immigrant, was an influential radical activist in the United States during the early twentieth century. She organized rallies and set up "No Conscription" leagues, designed to show popular protest against the policy of conscription, during World War I. Conscription, or compulsory enrollment in the military, was a practice employed during the war in both Europe and the United States. Goldman opposed this practice because she questioned America's motivation for going to war.

In the summer of 1917 Goldman was arrested for obstructing the draft and served two years in prison. After she had served her sentence, Goldman was stripped of her citizenship and was deported to Russia. In the following speech, given at an anticonscription meeting at the Harlem River Casino on May 18, 1917, Goldman strongly expresses opposition to the war and to conscription. This address was later cited as evidence against her in the anticonscription trial in June and July 1917. In her speech she blames the U.S. government and influential figures from Wall Street for America's entry into the war. Her references to Russia and the czar reflect the changes that that nation was undergoing as a result of the Russian Revolution, which was then taking place. Goldman concludes by stating that the general population needs to have a voice in this war, and she urges those who share her views to strike and to participate in protests.

Emma Goldman, address at the Harlem River Casino, May 18, 1917.

We don't believe in conscription, this meeting tonight being a living proof. This meeting was arranged with limited means. So, friends, we who have arranged the meeting are well satisfied if we can only urge the people of entire New York City and America, there would be no war in the United States—there would be no conscription in the United States—if the people are not given an opportunity to have their say. Therefore, we hope at least that a small portion of the population of New York City tonight is having its say.

We Need Democracy More than Germany

Friends, what I have to tell you tonight I want to impress upon your minds with all the intensity of my being, that we have with us people who came to break up this meeting, and therefore, friends, I ask you, friends, in the name of peace, in the name of freedom, and all that is dear to you, to be perfectly quiet, and when the meeting is over to leave the hall quietly, for that is a better argument than by the provocators who came here tonight to break up the meeting. Therefore, friends, I repeat once more, that after our speakers will be through, I hope you will leave the hall quietly, and, if there is the slightest trouble, we will hold the troublemakers, the provocators and the police responsible for the trouble.

Friends, I know perfectly well that tomorrow morning the daily papers will say that the German Kaiser [Wilhelm II] paid for this meeting. I know that they will say that those employed in the German service have arranged this meeting. But there is all of us, friends, who have something serious at hand—those of us to whom liberty is not a mere shadow—and found to be celebrated on the 4th of July, and to be celebrated with fire crackers—that we will not only speak for it, but die for it if necessary.

We are concerned in our own conscience, and we know that the meeting tonight has been arranged by working men and working women, who probably gave their last cent from their wages which the capitalistic regime is granting them.

And so, friends, we do not care what people will say

about us, we only care for one thing, and that is to demonstrate tonight and to demonstrate as long as we can be able to speak, that when America went into war, ostensibly for the purpose of fighting for democracy—because it is a dastardly lie—it never went into war for democracy. If it is true that America went into war in order to fight for democracy—why not begin at home? We need democracy. We need democracy even more than Germany, and I will tell you why. The German people were never brought up with the belief that they lived in democracy. The German people were nursed from their mothers' breasts that they were living in liberty and that they had all the freedom they desired. Therefore, the German people are not disappointed in the Kaiser. They have a Kaiser, the kind of a Kaiser they want and are going to stand for.

We in America have been brought up, we have been told that this is a free Republic. We have been told that free speech and free press and free assembly are guaranteed by the Constitution. Incidentally, friends, the only people who still believe in the Constitution are you poor fools for the other fellows. We are rather disappointed. When suddenly, out of the clear sky, a few months after we have been told he kept us out of war—we are now told he drew us into war.

We, who came from Europe, came here looking to America as the promised land. I came believing that liberty was a fact. And when we today resent war and resent conscription, it is not that we are foreigners and don't care, it is precisely because we love America and we are opposed to war.

We Refuse to Support a War for Money

My friends, when I say we love America, I wish you to remember that we don't love the American Wall Street, that we don't love the American [banker J.P.] Morgan, that we don't love the American [industrialist John D.] Rockefeller, we don't love the American Washington, we don't love the American ammunition manufacturers, we don't love the American National Security League—for that America is Russia transferred to America.

We mean the America of [antislavery leader] Wendell

Phillips, we mean [Ralph Waldo] Emerson, we mean America of great pioneers of liberty. We mean writers, and great men and women, who have fought for years to maintain the standard of effort. I, for one, am quite willing to stand up face to face with patriots every night—patriots blind to the injustice committed in this country—patriots who didn't care a hang. We are willing to stand up and to say to them: "Keep your dirty hands off America." You have no right to tell the people to give their lives in behalf of democracy, when democracy is the laughing stock before all Europe. And therefore, friends, we stand here and we tell you that the war which is now declared by America in the last six weeks is not a war of democracy and is not a war of the urging of the people. It is not a war of economic independence. It is a war for conquest. It is a war for military power. It is a war for money. It is a war for the purpose of trampling under foot every vestige of liberty that you people have worked for, for the last forty or thirty or twenty-five years and, therefore, we refuse to support such a war.

We are told, friends, that the people want war. If it is true that the American people want war, why not give the American people a chance to say whether they want war. Friends, we were told that the American people have a chance to say whether they want war through Congress and through the Senate. Congress is in the hands of those who pull the string. It is a jumping jack.

Friends, in Congress there are a few men in the Senate who wanted to keep America out of war. They have been hounded and persecuted and abused and insulted and degraded because they stood up for a principle. And so it was not true that the people of America have a chance to express its views. It was impossible, because each Congressman and each Senator is taken into a private room where spiritualistic mediums are being used, and they are mesmerized and massaged until every revolutionary fibre is out of them, and then they come out and do as they're told by the administration in Washington.

The same is true about conscription. What chance have you men, to say, if you men are to be conscripted. It took England eighteen months—a monarchy—to decide whether she shall have conscription. Up on the people born under a free sky—conscription has been imposed upon you. You cannot have democracy and have compulsory military training. You have become Russia. . . .

Now, friends, do you suppose for one minute that this Government is big enough and strong enough and powerful enough to stop men who will not engage in the war because they don't want the war, because they don't believe in the war, because they are not going to fight a war for Mr. Morgan? What is the Government going to do with them? They're going to lock them up—You haven't prisons enough to lock up all the people.

We Believe in Violence

We believe in violence and we will use violence. Remember, friends, that the very Government which worships at the altar of the Christian religion, that this very Government knows perfectly well, that they attempted to silence them. And so, if it is their intention to make us quiet, they may prepare the noose, they may prepare the gallows, they may build more prisons—for the spread of revolt and conscience.

How many people are going to refuse to conscript, and I say there are enough. I would count at least 50,000, and there are enough to be more, and they're not going to when only they're conscripted. They will not register.

I realize perfectly, that it is possible to gather up 50 and 100 and 500 people—and what are you going to do if you have 500,000 people? It will not be such an easy job, and it will compel the Government to sit up and take notice and, therefore, we are going to support, with all the means at our support with money and publicity—we are going to support all the men who will refuse to register and who will refuse to fight.

We want you to fill out these slips and as you go out drop them into the baskets at the door. We want to know how many men and women of conscriptive age—and they're going to take women and not soldiers. It is the same thing as if you fight in the war. Don't let them tell you that they will send you to the farm. Every stroke of what you do you are supporting the war, and the only reply that you can make against the war is that you are making men—that you are busy fighting your internal enemy, which is the capitalistic class.

I hope that this meeting is not going to be the first and last. As a matter of fact, we are planning something else.

Friends, listen, think of it. Not only are you going to be compelled—coerced—to wear the soldier's uniform, but on the day when you leave to be educated to the monster war, on the day when it will be decided that you shall be driven into the trenches and battlefield, on that day we are going to have a demonstration, but be careful whom—you might bury yourself and not the working class. We will have a demonstration of all the people who will not be conscripted and who will not register. We are going to have the largest demonstration this city has ever seen, and no power on earth will stop us.

I will say, in conclusion, that I, for one, am quite willing to take the consequences of every word I said and am going to say on the stand I am taking. I am not afraid of prison—I have been there often. It isn't quite so bad. I am not afraid of the authorities—I have dealt with them before—and rather, they have dealt with me, and am still living and stand here before you. I am not afraid of death. I would rather die the death of a lion than live the life of a dog.

We Represent the Future

For the cause of human liberty, for the cause of the working class, for the cause of men and women who live and till the soil—if I am to die for them, I could not wish a more glorious death ever in my wildest dreams. And so, patriots, and police, and gentlemen, who represent wealth and power, help yourself—you cannot stop the revolutionary spirit. It may take as long as one year or two. You cannot do it, because the spirit of revolution has a marvelous power of liberty. It can break through bars—it can go through safely. It can come out stronger and braver. If there is any man in this hall that despairs—let's look across Russia—let's look across: See the wonderful thing that revolution has done. It has thrown the Czar and his clique and his ever staunch henchmen into prison. It has opened Siberia and all the dungeons, and the men and women are going to be free. They are not going to be free according to American democracy.

Friends, I insist it is a good place for them in Russia. Let's go back home tomorrow. So, friends, don't be afraid. Take this marvelous meeting, take this wonderful spirit, and re-member that you are not alone—that tonight, in every city, in every hamlet and in every village and town, there are hearts beating that they don't want war, that they don't want conscription—that they are not going to be conscripted.

The ruling classes fight a losing game. The Wall Street men are fighting a losing game. They represented the past and we represent the future.

The future belongs to the young men, who are barely of age and barely realizing their freedom. The future belongs to the young girls and young boys. They must be free from mil-itarism. They must be free from the military yoke. If you want war, help yourself. Fight your own battle. We are not going to fight it for you.

So, friends, it is our decision tonight. We are going to fight for you, we are going to assist you and cooperate with you, and have the grandest demonstration this country has ever seen against militarism and war. What's your answer? Your answer to war must be a general strike, and then the governing class will have something on its hands.

An Allied Victory Means Freedom and Peace

Newton Baker

In March 1916 Newton Baker was appointed secretary of war by President Woodrow Wilson. He remained in that position until 1921. Although he had been a pacifist earlier in his career, Baker, while serving under Wilson, boosted American military preparedness on the eve of America's entry into World War I. He also devised military conscription plans that mobilized 4 million men in the United States.

Baker gave a number of pro-war speeches upon America's entry into the war. He described these addresses as spontaneous reflections based on current events. In a speech delivered on October 8, 1917, at a Liberty Loan meeting at Keith's Theater in Washington, D.C., Baker talks about the purpose of the war as an effort to spread democracy. He believes that alongside Great Britain and France, America will prevail in this war. He also considers the way in which the war will be remembered: as a victory at the front and a victory on the home front. Baker concludes by urging Americans to make financial contributions as a means of supporting the march toward liberty.

Newton Baker, address to a Liberty Loan meeting, Washington, DC, October 8, 1917.

In this center of the nation's activity; in this city [Washington, D.C.], which since we went into this war has perhaps doubled in population; in this city where the once peaceful beauty of a quiet capital has given place to almost feverish preparation and activity, there seem to be obvious lessons on every street and in every house, of the character of the task which the nation has assumed; and yet it is not inappropriate that a few words should be said that will give some comprehension, perhaps, of the size of that task and bring home its patriotic lesson to the people who are privileged to live thus close to the center of the nation's life.

The Verdict of History

For a thousand years, children will read in their books of history and the literature of the world will be enriched with the poetry and romance growing out of this age in which we live. The stories which will then be told are the history which is now being made, and I delight, in moments of idleness, to try to project myself into that remote and distant future and see the bent figure of some schoolboy as he pores over the history of this period; I think I can detect even in a boy so remote from the action of this time, the surge of enthusiasm in the things that the world is now doing.

I shall not undertake in the very brief time allotted for this address, to recount the history of the European War prior to our entrance into it nor the occasion for our entrance. But if there be anything certain about a contemporaneous estimate of the historical facts, the verdict of history will be that this, the first great free nation of the world—in this age the greatest nation in the world, in material resources, and in the progress she has made—was also the greatest nation on the face of the earth at this time in her moral quality and in the superb patience with which she endeavored to avert this catastrophe.

For long and weary months, with our minds daily harrowed and our hearts nightly torn with the stories of destruction, devastation, cruelty and despoliation of peoples everywhere, we still hoped against hope that the war could be brought to a conclusion, just to mankind and promising for future progress, without the unsheathing of our sword.

When, finally, after one bitter evidence had accumulated upon another, and we realized that this was really the final war of two great philosophies; and when we as Americans realized that the nations fighting on what we now call our side were really children of our spirit and baptized with the notion of liberty which we had fostered in this country for over a hundred years; and when we realized that England, France, Italy and Russia were fighting the battle not for selfish aggrandizement, but for liberty and opportunity, and for the philosophy of democracy on the part of the whole world, it became necessary for us to join with them in order to vindicate that philosophy.

The March Toward Liberty

On the bottom of the pathless ocean lie now the bones and the bodies of American men, women and children slain while we were still neutral, in defiance of every law that man ever ordained for the limitation of the horrors of war.[1] Our special grievance was only the occasion, and now that we are entered in this great conflict, we realize, with an inspiration that I think must fire every man, that this is merely the second stage in the march of the human race toward liberty. It began in 1776. In 1917 we pass the next milestone, and when it is passed, men and women everywhere will realize that no return of the Darker Age is possible; that victory has been won in this contest, autocracy having been demonstrated as too wasteful and too regardless of human life and human treasure to be tolerated, and democracy having been demonstrated to be not only the source of fruitful happiness and opportunity in time of peace, but to contain in itself the strength to survive. Having thus demonstrated the feebleness and viciousness of the principle of autocracy and the virility and salvation of the principle of democracy, we will start from a fresh platform with a new idea of its possibilities and a new hold upon permanent liberty and democratic institutions.

As a result, this country presents a strange but inspiring

1. This refers to the German sinking of the *Lusitania*.

spectacle. I have had some opportunity at Washington to participate in the formulation of plans, and out of Washington, I have had some opportunity to see the fruition of those plans. In sixteen places in this country cities have been built, as it seems, over night, housing great multitudes of people— thirty and forty thousand young men selected out of the body of our men; not in response to a sudden impulse of the military power, but selected by the civilian agencies of our people and presented to our government to be trained as a great army to participate in this reconquest of the world's liberty. Thus great cities have been built.

Where we used to spend five, ten or fifteen millions of dollars, we are now spending money that counts up in the billions. We are financing to some extent those associated with us in this war who have been long bearing the drain and strain of continuous warfare. We are spending money for munitions of war and for supplies, and our factories are responding with extraordinary energy. In workshops, factories, stores, the people of America have associated themselves in this great enterprise until our nation, our peaceful and peace-loving nation, is to-day knit together in spirit, more harmonious in its aspirations, more effective in its occupations. We are more of a nation to-day than we have been at any time in the whole hundred years and more of our glorious history.

Victory Together with France and England

I have stood at those camps and watched the boys who are preparing to be soldiers. I have seen them stream past by tens of thousands; some of them fresh-called to the colors from homes in remote places, far from the great rush of the world's events, some of them students from colleges; some of them engineers, men of occupations, professions, science; and as I have seen those youthful faces I have had a new realization of the springs of national action. As I saw those men I could not persuade myself that all of them were deeply read in the history of the world; I could not persuade myself that they knew the ultimate nature of this conflict of freedom with autocracy in the world; but there they marched with the sun shining on their faces, with flushed health in their cheeks, determination and a heroic quality about them that simply pervaded the atmosphere. And I realized that it is not necessary for a man to be a philosopher or a scholar to be a patriot, that there is something subtle in the very character of our soil that goes into the system of those born on it, and that this great army of young men reaching from the Pacific to the Atlantic, and now streaming across the Atlantic are men who possess that subtle quality and are filled with the spirit of patriotism, and that when our forces actually join with those on the other side the great battle will be won.

And that schoolboy a thousand years from now who reads the history of this age will read with admiration and throbbing heart of France—leader in the world's civilization, that country through which Guizot[2] said every great idea had to pass in order that it might be familiarized to the world— he will read of that France, not prepared for this sort of struggle, devoting herself to the redemption of her freedom and protection of her soul. When he comes to her glorious victory at the Marne, he will experience such a thrill as we used to feel as we read the story of Thermopylæ and Marathon. And when he comes to read of England he will have a realization of the English people which I think is slowly being brought home to us all. The English people speak of themselves as "muddling through"; but that schoolboy a thousand years from now will promptly see that that nation, with its terrible patience, was able to wait and coördinate its military and industrial strength until it arrived at a point, when it could and did, with the clocklike regularity, beat back the foe.

Then he will come to our entrance into the war, and coupling it up with what he has been reading before, he will go back to the origin of our liberty and see the people of this continent, having wrought out their own civilization, having elevated the individual man to a new dignity in world affairs, join the others, and he will realize that the victory will belong to the heroic quality of these united races.

He will ask whether all the war, all the victory was won

2. François Guizot was a nineteenth-century French statesman and historian.

at the front. He will find that war had become of such a quality that the fighting men are but part of a nation's army, that there is required to be at home in the field the grower of food and in the factory the maker of products, in order that the men at the front may fight; and that underlying the whole structure is the financial stability and the financial willingness of the people to fight the fight.

And so, with this opportunity to subscribe to Liberty Bonds [U.S. bonds issued to raise money for the war effort], we are appealing now to the very foundation of the nation's strength and the indispensable thing upon which its activities must rest, and we ask the people of the United States to sacrifice. I have had, since I have been Secretary of War, thousands of letters from high-spirited men and women all over the United States, from children nine and ten years old to men eighty and ninety, asking me "Where can I do my bit? What sacrifice can I make to advance this cause?" Some are too young and some are too old to fight, but none are too old or too young to sacrifice in this great financial effort, which is the basis upon which all must rest.

I can see victory ahead of us; a victory in arms, it is true, but a higher victory than that. I can see the American spirit, the unselfish, uncorrupted, untainted spirit of America with which we have gone into this struggle, dominant in the world as the result of that victory. I can see the peace that is to be made as the result of this great struggle; and it is a peace which brings us no selfish advantage, no national monopoly of the goods of the world, the possession of nobody else's goods and fortunes as the outcome, but an enkindling of a new spirit of justice; a peace after which the nations of the earth will join hands in harmonious cooperation rather than in selfish, deadly preparation for mutual destruction. And in order that there may be a war fought to a victorious conclusion, a peace so high and beneficent as that, those who are carrying forward this campaign ask you to pour out your money, not at the feet of the God of War, but into the lap of the Goddess of Liberty.

America Is Confident

Franklin K. Lane

Franklin K. Lane served as U.S. secretary of the interior under President Woodrow Wilson from 1913 to 1920. In this role, he toured many national parks and had the opportunity to speak with Americans throughout the country. Though born in Canada, Lane was at home in his adopted land and held many government positions. He made a number of speeches throughout World War I and stood firmly behind Wilson's effort.

On October 18, 1917, Lane made a speech in Philadelphia following a three-week trip to the western United States. Throughout the address he shares his experiences from the journey—and the encounters he had with westerners—to illustrate the unity among Americans in support of the war effort. As evidence, Lane cites the fact that throughout the nation people volunteer for military service and make financial contributions. Lane also states that the country is bound by a common determination to win the war. The war is a test, he says, in which the greatness of the United States will be proven.

I have just returned from a three weeks' trip throughout the West. I went from Louisiana through Oklahoma, Kansas, Colorado, Wyoming, Utah, Idaho, to Oregon. My journey was one of curiosity. I had been told that somewhere in far distant reaches of the continent the men and women of our country were disloyal to their flag, or at least

---

Franklin K. Lane, address in Philadelphia, October 18, 1917.

that they did not think enough of it to fight for it. Washington [D.C.], as some of you know, is a strange place. It is a cup, a valley surrounded by a horseshoe of mountains into which, by some strange law, the miasmic vapors of the country drop and set up strange states of mind. I was told in Washington that the only section of this country which was enlightened and patriotic enough to understand the deep significance of this war and to be willing to sacrifice for it was that fortunate section which borders on the Atlantic Ocean; that out beyond the hills to the westward were to be found limitless plains upon which lived those who, like some Buddhist monks of whom I have read, sat throughout the days in silent and solemn contemplation, their eyes centered on the pits of their stomachs, never looking up at the sky nor out upon the fields, and never hearing the voice of the world as it passed by—self-centered, flabby, spiritless. And so I went out beyond these western hills to find these strange creatures at this time. There are many hills between the Atlantic and the Pacific, and as I crossed one range after another I was told, "If there are any such people they are beyond the other range," until I came to the sea that looks out upon China. And I did not find those for whom I sought. I came back with the feeling that it was a good thing to leave Washington once in a while. This is a very great country that we live in. To know how great it is and to know its spirit one must not rest long in any one spot.

The Spirit of the West

I went to Oklahoma. There I had been told that I would find the very seat and center of hostility to the Government. I found there a few misled tenant farmers had objected to the draft. When I asked what reason they gave they said New York had brought on the war, and New York should make the fight. But that was not the spirit of Oklahoma, not nearly so much the spirit of Oklahoma as the draft riots were the spirit of New York in [18]'63. There is one town of 5000 people in Oklahoma who bought $275,000 worth of Liberty Bonds, more than one fifty-dollar bond for each inhabitant, man, woman and child, and who raised $18,000 for the Red

Cross, more than three dollars and a half for each inhabitant of the town. That does not look like slacking. After a meeting in Tulsa a man came to me, dressed in a blue jumper and overalls, and said: "Mr. Lane, I am doing my bit. I have six children, four boys and two girls. The four boys are in the Army and the two girls are Red Cross nurses, and I am saving to buy a Liberty Bond." That does not look like slacking either. In Salt Lake City I reviewed the newly organized troops, and the grandson of Brigham Young, who is a colonel of one of the regiments, pointed with justifiable pride to one of the companies that passed and said: "Every boy in that company has bought a Liberty Bond. They are not only willing to fight but they are willing to pay for their own support while they are fighting." In Idaho, ex-Governor Hawley took me into his library, and showed me the picture of four boys upon the wall, his sons, and said: "I am left all alone. All those boys have gone into the war." In Portland, Oregon, they told me that not one man had been drafted from that county, because the full quota of the county had been filled by men who volunteered for the regular army or militia. That is the spirit of the West. [British writer Rudyard] Kipling says that "East is East and West is West," but I say to you that there is neither East nor West to this country. It is one, bound by a common determination to win this war.

Another thing I found was that the people of the United States have entire confidence in President Woodrow Wilson, the Commander-in-Chief of the Army and the Navy. They believe that the President knows how to make war and when to make peace. They know that he is honest and that their money will not be wasted. They know that in the conduct of the war he has arisen above partisanship, above politics, into the high, clear air of patriotic statesmanship. The men that he asks for and the money that he asks for they will give. They may not know the intricacies of international law or the fine points of national pride, and may not even realize the significance to themselves and to the world of this momentous contest, but they know that President Wilson endured with patience, and came to his judgment solemnly and slowly. And they will follow wherever he leads and at the pace he wishes to go. They have seen moving pictures of the President marching at the head of the parade when the men from Washington marched to Fort Myer, and they like his stride.

America Has No Doubt of Itself

We are an impatient people. There are some who cannot understand why we do not have a million men in France at this moment. And when we ask them: "How would you get them there? Where are the ships to carry them? Where are the ships to munition them? Where are the ships to support them?" they have no answer. "We should have the ships," they say. I remember that Secretary [of Treasury William] McAdoo three years ago, within a month after the war broke out in Europe, advocated the construction of a great fleet of merchant ships by the Government or under Government guaranty. And if there was a voice raised in this city in favor of that program I failed to hear it. But we are going to have those ships. By next spring we will have one million tons of new shipping. By then we are promised the equivalent of two 5000-ton steamships per day, to continue indefinitely. And after the war we will restore the American flag to the seven seas of the world and enter into a generous rivalry with all Europe to sell our goods stamped "Made in America."

We are a critical people. Each one of us knows best how a thing should be done. Now I have no doubt that we have made mistakes and will make mistakes in preparation for and in the conduct of the war. There never yet was a railroad laid in the United States that did not have to have its lines changed after construction. Let me say this bluntly to you, that if this huge and unparalleled job cannot be done it will be because there are not men in the United States who can do it, for we have not hesitated to call upon those men who have proved themselves in the conduct of the greatest enterprises on this continent,—railroad presidents, engineers, chemists, contractors, manufacturers, inventors. The brains of the United States are involved in the conduct of this war. We have asked no man whether he is a Republican or a Democrat. We have not sought to know whether he was rich or poor. If he would serve the Nation at this time he was our man. And it is a matter of the profoundest pride to me and to every one who knows the facts that the business men of this country have not waited for the call but have volunteered in overwhelming numbers to give of their time and their capacity, without compensation, in this hour of the Government's need.

There is no thought throughout the country that we will not succeed either in raising the money or the men that we need. This country has no doubt of itself. It is the creature of faith. It is greater than any man and greater than any group of men. It is a great adventurous spirit. No man can look as I have done during the last three weeks on the enterprise and the industry and the wealth of this country and think for one moment that we can fail. I have passed through mile after mile of blazing forges. I have seen a solid mountain of the richest copper handled with a steam shovel. I have seen land that yielded sixty bushels of wheat to the acre and more land that yielded four hundred bushels of potatoes to the acre. We will not let our allies starve. We will not let them go without shot for their guns.

The Art of Cooperation

This task upon which we are engaged, it must be remembered, is the greatest enterprise that any nation has ever undertaken. For we have not only had to create an army, but we have had to help in the financing of four of the greatest nations of the world, to aid in the reconstruction of their railroads, in supplying them with munitions and with food, and this at a distance of more than three thousand miles. We have had to stimulate our own industries and our own agriculture. We have had to make plans for saving food and saving money, for the protection of our own people as well as others against profiteering. Each day there have been prophesies of failure, but our Navy patrols the sea, and not a man has been lost on his way to France; our Army is housed, clothed, and is in the field drilling, and we are getting rifles for them at the rate of fifteen thousand a day.

The message that the West sends to you is this: Have faith in your country, have faith in your Government, remember that prophesies of evil always fail in the United States. Whatever the temporary conditions may be, the man who is the thoroughbred wins out. We are but beginning to learn the art of coöperation in the United States. We have not exercised the powers as a government that can be exercised for the support and maintenance of the great enterprises and industries of the country which are its arteries, its hands and feet. Go out over the western hills and you will come back, as I have come back, without depression, with a heart full of confidence in the robust spirit, the manly determination and the fine idealism of our people, as well as in their ability to put at the service of the world the unending resources of this great continent. The stock ticker is not a stalwart boy in khaki, filled with courage and proud to do his bit for a country that he loves—no, the stock ticker is a nervous old man who sometimes thinks himself the master of the world and again fears his own shadow. It has not conscience, courage or vision. It may be a thermometer but it is not a seer. . . .

This is to be a grim time for us. Let us not delude ourselves or carry any false illusions that the righteousness of our cause, the injustice done to us, the vastness of our resources, or the greatness of our man-power will so touch or overawe the enemy as to make them seek a peace that will make this world safe for Democracy until those who have forced this fight realize that with the world against them they cannot win. [British prime minister David] Lloyd George said the other day that the United States had never fought a war that it had not won. He might have added that we never fought a war in which we did not know that we were right. This war, however, is to be a supreme test. We are to test the fiber of our people; we are to test our ability to coöperate; we are to test our sense of nationalism; we are to test our loyalty to Democracy; we are to test to the ultimate the resources of our nation, the capacity of our mines and miners, of our farms and farmers, of our mills and millhands. We are to test our vision and the greatness of our own minds—whether we are worthy of a large future or wedded to a little life; we are to test our own conception of this country and its relation to the world.

What is to be the future of the United States? It was not in the nature of things that we could remain isolated. It was our hope that this might be so, but seas have narrowed and interests have been so twisted and intertwined, and our rights are so identical with the right of others that the world had become before this war a great Brotherhood. We made rules to control this relationship. Each people was to determine for itself what its own internal policy should be.

It was not for us to say that the form of government which best pleased us should be adopted by others. But it was for us to say that, notwithstanding we were a democracy, notwithstanding our isolated position, removed from the European and Asiatic world of struggle, we must be treated with full national honors and rights. The first condition of that Brotherhood was that each member of it should regard his given word as a pledge upon which turned his right to recognition and fraternity. Upon entering into this war, Germany violated that pledge by the invasion of Belgium. She tore her treaty up and gave notice to the world that her war necessities were superior to her national word. That was a shock to the conscience of every people. But we stood neutral because we did not realize then, as we did later, that this act was but an evidence of a policy which must sooner or later affect rights in which we were vitally interested. We saw the German army march to within fifty miles of Paris, until old Marshal Joffre [supreme commander of the French armies until 1916] stood on the Marne and said: "This has gone far enough." We made no protest at the invasion of the country which had followed our lead into democracy. Then Germany turned to the seas. She sank our boats loaded with American grain, and we contented ourselves with a protest. She sank the *Lusitania* carrying American civilians. We protested that the seas belonged to us as much as to her; that for a thousand years the lives of civilians had been regarded as sacred, even though on an enemy ship. And no apology came. One after another our ships went down and the ships of other neutral nations. Lives by the hundreds were lost. She promised to respect our rights, but after a time, when she had become ready to carry on in more ruthless fashion her predatory war upon the seas, we found that this promise was as worthless to us as her promise to Belgium had been to her. Then, by the power vested in it by the Constitution, Congress declared that war had been made upon us and accepted the challenge which Germany had thrown down. We were no longer to be regarded as a nation of cowards who would not enforce recognition of what all nations had conceded to be our rights. There is no appeal from that decision. It is idle to argue to-day as to the cause of the war. It it equally idle to argue that we should not have entered the war. We have made our decision and we are going forward. We know that we are right. Our conscience would have convicted us of cowardice if we had longer withheld the assertion of our power.

This Is a War of Principles

But this war has grown away from a mere invasion of our rights. It is to-day a contest between the principle of empire and the principle of democracy—a contest between the few who believe in government by the soldier and the many who believe in government by the people. It is a contest between those who believe that men are made to serve the government and those who believe that government is made to serve the people. It is a contest between those who believe that the purpose of a government is to enrich itself by extending its boundaries through the use of force, and those who believe that the purpose of government is to insure to the people life, liberty, and the pursuit of happiness. Two systems are in conflict here. The one has come down to us from Cæsar. It believes in mastery, in fear, in power. The other is the outgrowth of a Christian civilization. It believes that no man or set of men have been created by God to master all men.

Why is the world against Germany? Germany does not know that the time of empires and emperors is past. She does not know that the day of arbitrary might has gone by. She will not play the Twentieth Century game under Twentieth Century rules. She asks for friendship, but she dishonors her friends by asking them to do things which they should not do. There was no country more willing to remain neutral than the Argentine Republic. Yet Germany's minister asks the Swedish minister to convey messages to Germany which outline a policy of ruthlessness upon the sea against that Republic which offends the sensibilities of mankind. You say to me that Germany was not hostile to the United States. How can any such statement be made in the face of the Zimmermann note, in which Germany, while we are still at peace with her, called upon Mexico as her friend to invade our territory, promising her as reward part of our own lands and attempting to induce her to involve Japan with her in war against us. . . .

Government by fear is not to be the master of this earth. If Germany succeeds, that is the only kind of government we will know. We will sail the seas by her consent, carrying our goods where she permits. We will live with a country filled with spies and with our national capital undermined by foreign intrigue. We will never be sure of the word that nations give to us. We will endure life with the horrors of another such war constantly in our minds. We will pay taxes unending and huge to support an army which we do not want but must have. Our sons will be raised with the constant thought in their minds that theirs is not the mission to reclaim the land, to dig the mine, to carry out the experiment, to lay the railroad, to lead the minds of men, to master the forces of unwilling nature; for, from this hope, this dream of usefulness, they may any day be turned aside by the stern necessity of self-protection; and their wives may be raised with the picture continually before their eyes of what has befallen the Belgian women. This is not a life for a self-respecting people. We must know where we are and what our standing is and what our future may be. We must know that we have rights upon this world—rights that do not depend upon sufferance, rights that we can assert. And we must know that while, we observe the common laws that govern mankind and keep our pledged word, no nation has in its mind the purpose to make us subject to a government that is not of our own making. This is the foundation stone of Americanism.

The Workers Support the War

Samuel Gompers

Samuel Gompers was president of the American Federation of Labor (AFL) from 1886 to 1924. The AFL is an organization of trade unions in the United States that provides workers with a means to express their political and economic concerns. During World War I Gompers aimed to unite organized labor behind the war effort. He was an early supporter of both President Woodrow Wilson and the decision to enter the war. Gompers organized the War Committee on Labor, and at the peace conference upon conclusion of the war, he served on the Commission on International Labor Legislation.

In a speech delivered at the Lexington Avenue Theater in New York on February 22, 1918, Gompers speaks of his transformation from pacifist to supporter of the war. Germany provoked the United States into war, he maintains. He notes that when government officials declared war upon Germany, it was a decision supported by the American people. Gompers also links the struggle for democracy abroad with organized labor's domestic crusade for democracy in the workplace. The workforce in the United States, Gompers pledges, will do its part in the war and make the necessary sacrifices. He emphasizes that organized labor is fully committed to victory.

Samuel Gompers, address at the Lexington Avenue Theater, New York, February 22, 1918.

I doubt that there existed, or now exists, in all the world a man who is so pronounced a pacifist as was I. I belonged to every peace society of which I knew anything. An officer in some form or other of each of them, a speaker of nearly all of them, within the sphere of my opportunities. In addition, as a union man, a labor man, an internationalist in spirit, I had believed, came to believe, that it would be impossible for such a war to have occurred at any time after the international understandings and pledge of the workers of nearly all the civilized countries; and I really believed in the pledge, in the spirit of it. . . . I had permitted myself to live in a fool's paradise. I believed that when men solemnly pledged themselves and those in whose name they had the authority to speak, they would go the limit in their own countries to prevent a rupture of international peace. . . . I was so in love with peace that I could have, without flinching, died for the cause of peace.

No Longer a Pacifist

Almost out of the clear sky came this declaration of war, and I found the men who had pledged to me and mine, my fellows, flying to the colors of the greatest autocrat of all time, the modern buccaneer of the world, the type of the intellectual scientific murderer, to fly to the colors upon his order, to attack the brothers whose lives they vouched to protect. I awoke. From then until now and until the peace of the world is assured I count myself transformed from an ultra pacifist to a living, breathing, fighting man. No one who has known me fairly intimately has ever accused me of running away from an honorable contest. And it is not of much interest what any one man believes or is, but that which he tries to inculcate upon his fellow-citizens. I believe that in our country we have the greatest opportunities existing of any country upon the face of the globe. America is not perfect; the Republic of the United States is not perfect; it has the imperfections of the human; and inasmuch as we are not perfect, we have not been able to make a perfect, democratic Republic; but it is the best country on the face of the earth.

America is not merely a name. It is not merely a land. It is not merely a country, nor is it merely a continent. America is a symbol; it is an ideal, the hopes of the world can be expressed in the ideal—America. The man in America, with the opportunities afforded, with the right of expression, with the right of determination, with the right of creating a political revolution by well-ordered methods, who will not or does not appreciate that it is his duty to stand by such a country in such stress and in such a storm, who is unwilling to stand up and be counted as a man in this fight for the maintenance of these ideals—is unworthy of the privilege of living in this country.

I have no quarrel with the man or the group of men who differ with me, or the course which I pursue, in anything. I doubt that there is anyone who welcomes expressions of dissent or disapproval more than I do. I am willing to battle with him mentally, argumentatively, in any honorable way that is provided among men, self-respecting men and women. Constructive criticism is of the greatest benefit to those who are criticized. It is the nagger, the mean, contemptible, nagging one that has no purpose other than negative and destructive that is unworthy the consideration of decent men and women.

The American People Support This War

Who declared war in Germany? Was it even that mugwumpery called the Reichstag [German parliament]? No; not even that. But who declared war in Germany? Was it the people of Germany? No. It was the Kaiser [Wilhelm II] and his immediate military clique. That autocratic clique by one accord determined that the time for which they had been planning had arrived, and then was the time to strike the blow. Now, you have no need to enter into a full discussion of all the matter which may be of vital interest, and no doubt you know them just as well, if not better, than I do, but here is the point: In the United States of America it was not a Kaiser, a King, or even the President of the United States who declared war; it was the Congress of the United States, the men and women elected by the people of the United States. There must be lodged somewhere in the Government the power to declare that its life is endangered and therefore has the right to strike a blow in the defense of that country. In our Republic that authority is vested in the Congress of the United States—the Congress elected by the people of the United States, the Congress elected, in many States, by the votes of the men and the women of those States. . . .

In truth, the state of war existed from January 1916, when the attacks were made upon our industrial plants and our transportation lines, the murdering of our men and women and our children in cold blood. If that did not constitute a state of war I would like to know what did. The point that I want to make clear is this: That it was not an autocrat, it was not the President, but that it was the representatives of the people, elected by the people to the Congress of the United States, the only authority recognized by the Constitution of our country, who realized the situation as it was and declared that a state of war existed between our Republic and the Imperial German Government. That body authorized the President to use all the available means and all the forces of the country to carry into effect and purpose the resolution of the Congress of the United States, and to make good this declaration that the democracy of the United States is not impotent or incompetent to defend itself.

Until the only authority in the country had decided the question whether we should recognize that war existed or not, until that declaration was made it was the privilege, as it was the right of every man to express his own view whether we should recognize this fact and go to war or not. But when the constituted authority in our Republic declared war, that was a decision of the people of this country, and from that decision there is and can be no appeal. To follow the thought that it is now permissible to discuss whether we should continue in the war or to retreat from it reminds me of the situation as it now exists in Russia.

An Atmosphere of Freedom

I think that every American, every liberty-loving man and woman throughout the whole world, was thrilled when we learned that the Russian people had overthrown the Czar and his Empire and established a Government based upon some sort of democratic conception. Not long after, under the leadership of so-called radicals, they undertook to institute in the army the democratic thought that before any battle was to be undertaken the soldiers should vote upon it. In theory that might be fairly good. As an academic discussion, it does not sound bad; but when you have opposed to you a well-organized gang of scientific murderers who have their guns leveled at you, that is not the time to discuss whether you should defend yourself or not. That is the time to fight. . . . Anarchy prevails in Russia, and the radicalism of the Bolsheviki of Russia has given the people, not land, not bread, not peace; and instead of finding this great people of Russia standing erect and fighting for their homes and for their lives, we find them without power or will, helpless before the Kaiser's hordes and the forces of autocracy, powerless to maintain their own freedom or to realize their own ideals. Yes, this radical, this radical gang there, and those who are showing their heads here, to them must be laid the charge of the undoing of the great people of Russia. If the so-called radicals of America would have their way, you would find in our United States the same condition as it is in Russia now.

I am rather fond of life. I have had 68 years of it, and I am not tired of it at all. I want to live. I don't know of anything better than living. I am not anxious to find out, but I don't want to live when I can't maintain my own self-respect. Indeed, I feel that I could not live in the atmosphere of unfreedom. There have been at least two occasions in my life when I was threatened with imprisonment; on two different occasions, and each for a year, because I undertook to express my judgment, and we were then at peace, not at war. But I undertook to express my judgment, express my opinion as an American citizen against a decree issued by one of our courts in a private controversy between two interests. I merely mention it, as I was willing to take a chance, whatever that may mean, for the maintenance of the principles of freedom of expression and freedom of the press.

So, just imagine—it does not take much to see the point at issue—if the German militarist system could win—it can't, but if it could win, how would that victory he accomplished, or what would its immediate result be? I know that we have been living in the thought that we are so far removed from the whole world that we are perfectly safe. But if it were possible for the German militarist machine to be so efficient that it could conquer France and England, the first result of that conquest would be, without question, the taking over from France and England of their combined navies. Without taking over these navies, as the result of German conquest, she could not be the complete winner; and imagine, with the military forces, the navies of England and France, and her vessels of commerce and transports, what would become of the vaunted safety of the home and fireside of the American people? . . .

We Are Fighting to Maintain Democracy at Home

To me this war has quite a different meaning than almost any other war in history of which I have read. It began through the machinations of the German Kaiser and in the splendid responses made by France and England and Belgium. In Prussia they were all exulting, but when the Republic of the United States entered into this world struggle it ceased to be a war and became at once a crusade for freedom and justice and liberty. I hold it to be the duty of every man to give every ounce of energy in fighting, in producing, in helping in any way that he can, that this crusade shall be a triumph for the world. If we may not be able to abolish war for all time, at least let us make the conditions such that a war of this character may never again occur, or at least shall be long deferred.

For years and years the workers of America, realizing the position in which we are placed in this most favored country of ours, pressed home upon the agencies of government, the agencies of industry, the agencies of all activities, that inasmuch as the workers performed so large a service for society and civilization, the human side of the workers should receive the highest consideration, and that no agency of government or of industry should be constituted without the representative of the workers as part of that agency.

I never have asked anything for myself. I have no favor to ask. I have no personal pleas to make. I speak for a cause. I speak for the masses of workers as well as the masses of all our people. For, no matter, the meanest of all of them, I consider it my duty and privilege to say a word for him, even when perhaps he might repudiate me. But, as the result of this war or crusade, this principle for which labor has been contending has found recognition in the department of government.

My friends, do you know how thoroughly in sympathy with the high and noble thought and work and associations of the labor movement are the members of the President's Cabinet and the President of the United States himself? That has come and it is coming to a larger extent with every development of our time. Does anyone think that when peace shall have come again to our beloved country and to the people of the world the representatives of these various agencies will be in conflict? Surely not. The principle is recognized. Hence this means while we are fighting for democracy and against autocracy, in France and soon in Belgium and then into Germany, then in the meantime we are fighting to maintain democracy at home.

The Workers Endorse the War Effort

Let me say to you that, talking of international conferences with representatives of the enemy countries, we are not going to permit ourselves to be lulled into a fancied security and, under the guise of radicalism, go back a hundred years. Why, the Kaiser's minions would not give a passport to anyone unless he would carry out the policy of the autocracy of Germany. . . .

One of the great causes of this was the obsession of this German military caste that democracies are impotent and inefficient; that France was a sort of democracy, with an army that was in a way inefficient because of the long-standing contention of Alsace-Lorraine. Germany knew that if she went to war she would have a rather hard fight with France, but surely would conquer her. She had an extreme contempt for the democracy of Great Britain and for any army Great Britain could raise. To the German mind, as it has been tutored for this last half a century, there is nothing efficient except it is governmental, unless it is directed by an autocratic head. The same contempt the Germans had for America. They believed us to be such devotees and lovers of the almighty dollar that we could never stand for an ideal and make sacrifices for its achievement. That is the great mistake which autocracies have ever made—they do not know. They have never known that once touch the heart, the conscience, and the spirit of the democratic peoples, they will make more sacrifices than any conscripts under compulsion. So we find ourselves in this war, in this crusade.

A month before the war was declared, with some degree of prescience, the executive council of the American Federation of Labor called a conference of the representative officials of the American labor movement, and there a great discussion ensued, and there a declaration was finally adopted. I am going to ask you to let me read the closing two paragraphs.

> We, the officers of the national and international trade-unions of America, in conference assembled, in the Capital of our Nation, hereby pledge ourselves, in peace or in war, in stress or in storm, to stand unreservedly by the standard of liberty and the safety and preservation of the institutions and ideals of our Republic. In this solemn hour of our Nation's life it is our earnest hope that our Republic may be safeguarded in its unswerving desire for peace; that our people may be spared the horrors and the burden of war; that they may have the opportunity to cultivate and develop the arts of peace, human brotherhood, and a higher civilization; but despite all our endeavors and hopes should our country be drawn into the maelstrom of the European conflict, we, with these ideals of liberty and justice herein declared as the indispensable basis for national policies, offer our services to our country in every field of activity to defend, safeguard, and preserve the Republic of the United States of America against its enemies, whomsoever they may be, and we call upon our fellow workers and fellow citizens in the holy name of labor, justice, freedom, and humanity to devotedly and patriotically give like service.

That declaration was adopted by a unanimous vote a month before the declaration of war. At the convention of the American Federation of Labor in November [1917], the President of the United States, that great leader and spokesman of the democracies of the world came and delivered a message to labor, and through that body, to the great masses of the people of America, and through them to the liberty-loving men and women of the whole world. Did you ever think, my friends, of the curious situation in our country? The Government of the country carrying on this war are unanimously pacifists, from the President, the Secretary of the Navy [Joseph Daniels], the Secretary of War [Newton Baker], the Secretary of Labor [William B. Wilson]—all of them ultrapacifists—before the war.

Worthy Sacrifices

If a gang of organized assassins were to come into this community, ready to pounce upon the innocent people, and they came upon the block in which you lived, and attacked your neighbor on the corner, what kind of a man would you be if you didn't get up and at them, rather than wait until they came into your own room? That is the situation with our country and our people in this great world struggle. There is not anything that will contribute so much to winning this war as the unity of spirit as well as the unity of action among the people of our country to make, if necessary, the extreme sacrifice that freedom shall live. I know that it may mean much loss and many heartaches, but we know that there were sacrifice and heartaches among the men and the women of our revolutionary times.

Who is there in America to-day who looks back with regret on the sacrifices made when the Declaration of Independence was coined for the world and a new nation created? Who regrets that anyone belonging to them, no matter how near or how remote, sacrificed his life and his all that America should be born? The war of our civilized life, our Civil War, when the struggle was for the maintenance of the Union and the abolition of human slavery, who among the gallant men on both sides, or either side, now regrets that the fight was made and the sacrifices borne in order to make good that this Nation is one and indivisible and that on its shores and under its flag slavery is forever abolished? Who doubts that? Our war with Spain, small though it was, meant sacrifices. It meant Cuba free and independent. Is there a man or woman in this audience or in this country who regrets the sacrifice that was made that Cuba might be made free?

So the men and the women of the future will regard this struggle as we now look upon those struggles to which I have just referred. They will call us blessed, every man and every woman, who has given something to this great cause of human justice and freedom, to feel the satisfaction, the exultation, the exaltation of youth and energy renewed in them in a great cause, the greatest that has ever been presented to the peoples of any country and in any time. It is a privilege to live in this time and to help in this common fight.

With all my heart and spirit I appeal to my fellow citizens, to my fellow workers, to make this one great slogan, the watchword from now on until triumph shall perch upon our arms: "Unity, solidarity, energy, and the will to fight and to win."

Peacemaking

America and Great Britain Are Brothers in a Common Cause

Rudyard Kipling

Rudyard Kipling, born in India to British parents in 1865, became a famous short-story writer and poet. During World War I he wrote a number of books supporting the Allied cause. The war also touched him personally. His only son was killed at the Battle of Loos in France in 1915 while serving with the Irish Guards. In the years following the war, Kipling searched vainly for his son's body in order to give him a proper burial.

Kipling strongly supported the Allied effort throughout the war. In the following address, delivered on July 21, 1918, to American troops at Winchester, England, Kipling extends gratitude to the United States for its help in the war. He considers Americans to be blood brothers in the struggle against Germany, which he believes is headed for defeat. Kipling also reflects upon the postwar world. His words have an ironic and amusing tone, and his anti-Germany stance is clearly presented. He states that Great Britain, France, and the United States will win the war. Then it will be the task of those nations to change Germany's militaristic, warlike heart and mind. Kipling maintains that this must be achieved in the interest of mankind.

Rudyard Kipling, address to American troops, Winchester, England, July 21, 1918.

Several years have passed since England was permanently occupied by the armed forces of a foreign nation. On the last occasion—eight hundred years ago—our people did not take kindly to the invaders. I know they did not, because I live a few miles from where the Battle of Hastings was fought, where all the trouble began; and I assure you we are still talking about it. But don't let me take up your time by retailing the local gossip of these parts. Besides, conditions have changed. They will after 853 years—even in England. You may have noticed that we natives do not resent either the presence of your armed forces on our soil, or your buildings such as these—huts, which are one of the visible signs of your occupation. As far as you are concerned, we are a placid, not to say pacifist, community. Why, gentlemen, you could not annoy us if you started in to build pyramids. On the contrary, we should be pleased. We should say: "This looks like business; this looks as if the United States meant to stay till they had done their share of the job thoroughly."

The Fight Against Germany

We have been a long time over our present job, and we may be a long time yet. It has been a little bigger than we expected, because this is the first time since the creation that all the world has been obliged to unite for the purpose of fighting the devil.[1] You remember that before the war one of our easy theories was that the devil was almost extinct—that he was only the child of misfortune or accident, and that we should soon abolish him by passing ringing resolutions against him. That has proved an expensive miscalculation. We find now that the devil is very much alive, and very much what he always was—that is to say, immensely industrious, a born organizer, and better at quoting [biblical] Scripture for his own ends than most honest men. His industry and organization we all can deal with, but more difficult to handle is his habit of quoting Scripture as soon as he is in difficulties.

When Germany begins to realize her defeat is certain we shall be urged in the name of mercy, toleration, loving kind-

---

1. Kipling refers here to Kaiser Wilhelm II.

ness, for the sake of the future of mankind, or by similar appeals to the inextinguishable vanity of man, who delights in thinking himself holy and righteous when he is really only lazy or tired—I say, we shall be urged on these high grounds to make some sort of compromise with or to extend some recognition to the power which has for its one object the destruction of man body and soul. Yet, if we accept these pleas, we shall betray mankind as effectively as though we had turned our backs upon the battle from the first.

But you, gentlemen, have not come 3000 miles to protect Germany. Your little vanguard is here to help her change her heart, and I read a day or two ago the line on which you propose to change it: "When we went to war with Germany it was with the resolve to destroy German war power. If that power is inseparable from the German people, then we are resolved upon the destruction of the German people. The alternative is in their hands." That is reasonable and easy to understand. You are going, none too soon, into a world which has been laboriously wrecked by high German philosophy, based on the devil's own creed that there is nothing good or evil in life but thinking makes it so—in other words, that right and wrong are matters of pure fancy.

We Are Blood-Brothers in a Common Cause

That belief it will be your privilege to assist in removing from the German's mind. His beliefs are primitive. Except on certain portions of the front, where he has been better educated, he believed that the United States Army does not exist. In the first place, it could not cross the Atlantic; in the second, it was sunk while crossing; in the third, it was no use when it arrived. It is possible that you may be able to persuade him that he has been misinformed on these points.

Meantime, your invasion of England goes forward according to program day by day. Unlike the other invaders we have known, you bring everything you need with you, and do not live upon the inhabitants. In this you are true to the historical vow of your ancestors, when they said to ours, "Millions for defense, but not a cent for tribute." At any other time the nations would be lost in amazement at the mere volume and scope of your equipment, at the terrifying completeness of your preparations, at the dread evidence of power that underlies them. But we have lived so among miracles these last four years that, even though the thing accomplished itself before our very eyes, we scarcely realize that we watch the actual bodily transit of the New World moving in arms to aid in redressing the balance of the Old. We are too close to these vast upheavals and breakings forth to judge of their significance. One falls back on the simpler, the more comprehensible fact that we are all blood-brothers in a common cause, and therefore in that enduring fellowship of loss, toil, peril, and homesickness which must needs be our portion before we come to the victory.

But life is not all gray even under these skies. There is a reasonable amount of fun left in the world still, if you know where to look for it—and I have noticed that the young generally have this knowledge. And there are worse fates in the world than to be made welcome, as you are more than welcome, to the honorable and gallant fraternity of comrades-in-arms the wide world over. Our country and our hearts are at your service, and with these our understanding of the work ahead of you. That understanding we have bought at the price of the lifeblood of a generation.

Germany Is Responsible for the War

Raymond Poincaré

On November 11, 1918, an armistice ending the fighting of World War I was reached after Germany asked for peace. In January 1919 the Paris Peace Conference opened and discussions began about the postwar world. Russia was not a participant in the peace conference. It had withdrawn from the war and made a separate peace with Germany in March 1918. None of the Central Powers, notably Germany and Austria-Hungary, were represented at the peace talks. Great Britain, France, the United States, Italy, and their allies negotiated over Germany's obligations as a defeated nation. The conference resulted in the Treaty of Versailles, which imposed on Germany financial reparations, losses of territory, and military restrictions. The Versailles treaty was signed on June 28, 1919, exactly five years after the assassination of Archduke Francis Ferdinand, the event that led to the war's outbreak.

The first general session of the Paris Peace Conference met on January 18, 1919, at the Quai d'Orsay. President Raymond Poincaré of France formally convoked the conference and gave the following inaugural address. He maintains that Germany alone was responsible for the war, and that the Allies worked together to save humankind from the German menace. He calls for harsh measures toward Germany, the future security of France, and the protection of free and newly independent nations.

Raymond Poincaré, Inaugural Address, January 18, 1919.

Poincaré reminds the conference participants that they are charged with establishing a new order to guarantee international safety and stability.

Gentlemen:—France greets and welcomes you and thanks you for having unanimously chosen as the seat of your labors the city [Paris] which, for over four years, the enemy has made his principal military objective and which the valor of the Allied armies has victoriously defended against unceasingly renewed offensives.

Allow me to see in your decision the homage of all the nations that you represent towards a country which, still more than any others, has endured the sufferings of war, of which entire provinces, transformed into vast battlefields, have been systematically wasted by the invader, and which has paid the heaviest tribute to death.

France has borne these enormous sacrifices without having incurred the slightest responsibility for the frightful cataclysm which has overwhelmed the universe, and at the moment when this cycle of horror is ending, all the Powers whose delegates are assembled here may acquit themselves of any share in the crime which has resulted in so unprecedented a disaster. What gives you authority to establish a peace of justice is the fact that none of the peoples of whom you are the delegates has had any part in injustice. Humanity can place confidence in you because you are not among those who have outraged the rights of humanity.

There is no need of further information or for special inquiries into the origin of the drama which has just shaken the world. The truth, bathed in blood, has already escaped from the Imperial archives. The premeditated character of the trap is to-day clearly proved. In the hope of conquering, first, the hegemony of Europe and next the mastery of the world; the Central Empires, bound together by a secret plot, found the most abominable pretexts for trying to crush Serbia and force their way to the East. At the same time they disowned the most solemn undertakings in order to crush Belgium and force their way into the heart of France. These are the two unforgetable outrages which opened the way to aggression. The combined efforts of Great Britain, France, and Russia broke themselves against that mad arrogance.

If, after long vicissitudes, those[1] who wished to reign by the sword have perished by the sword, they have but themselves to blame; they have been destroyed by their own blindness. What could be more significant than the shameful bargains they attempted to offer to Great Britain and France at the end of July, 1914, when to Great Britain they suggested: "Allow us to attack France on land and we will not enter the Channel"; and when they instructed their Ambassador to say to France: "We will only accept a declaration of neutrality on your part if you surrender to us Briey, Toul, and Verdun." It is in the light of these memories, gentlemen, that all the conclusions you will have to draw from the war will take shape.

Your nations entered the war successively, but came, one and all, to the help of threatened right. Like Germany, Great Britain and France had guaranteed the independence of Belgium. Germany sought to crush Belgium. Great Britain and France both swore to save her. Thus, from the very beginning of hostilities, came into conflict the two ideas which for fifty months were to struggle for the dominion of the world—the idea of sovereign force, which accepts neither control nor check, and the idea of justice, which depends on the sword only to prevent or press the abuse of strength.

The Allies Worked Together

Faithfully supported by her Dominions and Colonies, Great Britain decided that she could not remain aloof from a struggle in which the face of every country was involved. She has made, and her Dominions and Colonies have made with her, prodigious efforts to prevent the war from ending in the triumph of the spirit of conquest and the destruction of right.

Japan, in her turn, only decided to take up arms out of loyalty to Great Britain, her great Ally, and from the consciousness of the danger in which both Asia and Europe

1. Germans

would have stood, for the hegemony of which the Germanic Empires had dreamt.

Italy, who from the first had refused to lend a helping hand to German ambition, rose against an age-long foe only to answer the call of oppressed populations and to destroy at the cost of her blood the artificial political combination which took no account of human liberty.

Rumania resolved to fight only to realize that national unity which was opposed by the same powers of arbitrary force. Abandoned, betrayed, and strangled, she had to submit to an abominable treaty,[2] the revision of which you will exact. Greece, whom the enemy for many months tried to turn from her traditions and destinies, raised an army only to escape attempts at domination, of which she felt the growing threat. Portugal, China, and Siam [Thailand] abandoned neutrality only to escape the strangling pressure of the Central Powers. Thus it was the extent of German ambitions that brought so many peoples, great and small, to form a league against the same adversary.

And what shall I say of the solemn resolution taken by the United States in the spring of 1917 under the auspices of their illustrious President, Mr. Wilson, whom I am happy to greet here in the name of grateful France, and if you will allow me to say so, gentlemen, in the name of all the nations represented in this room? What shall I say of the many other American Powers which either declared themselves against Germany—Brazil, Cuba, Panama, Guatemala, Nicaragua, Haiti, Honduras—or at least broke off diplomatic relations—Bolivia, Peru, Ecuador, Uruguay? From north to south the New World rose with indignation when it saw the empires of Central Europe, after having let loose the war without provocation and without excuse, carry it on with fire, pillage, and massacre of inoffensive beings?

The intervention of the United States was something more, something greater, than a great political and military event: it was a supreme judgment passed at the bar of history

---

2. The Treaty of Bucharest of 1918 between Romania and the Central Powers called for Romanian demobilization and the cession of Romanian territory. Romania later rejected ratification of the treaty.

by the lofty conscience of a free people and their Chief Magistrate on the enormous responsibilities incurred in the frightful conflict which was lacerating humanity. It was not only to protect themselves from the audacious aims of German megalomania that the United States equipped fleets and created immense armies, but also, and above all, to defend an ideal of liberty over which they saw the huge shadow of the Imperial Eagle encroaching farther every day. America, the daughter of Europe, crossed the ocean to wrest her mother from the humiliation of thraldom and to save civilization. The American people wished to put an end to the greatest scandal that has ever sullied the annals of mankind.

Free Peoples Are Represented Here

Autocratic governments, having prepared in the secrecy of the Chancelleries and the General Staff a map program of universal domination, at the time fixed by their genius for intrigue let loose their packs and sounded the horns for the chase, ordering science at the very time when it was beginning to abolish distances, bring men closer, and make life sweeter, to leave the bright sky towards which it was soaring and to place itself submissively at the service of violence, lowering the religious idea to the extent of making God the complacent auxiliary of their passions and the accomplice of their crimes; in short, counting as naught the traditions and wills of peoples, the lives of citizens, the honor of women, and all those principles of public and private morality which we for our part have endeavored to keep unaltered throughout the war and which neither nations nor individuals can repudiate or disregard with impunity.

While the conflict was gradually extending over the entire surface of the earth, the clanking of chains was heard here and there, and captive nationalities from the depth of their agelong jails cried out to us for help. Yet more, they escaped to come to our aid. Poland came to life again and sent us troops. The Czecho-Slovaks won their right to independence in Siberia, in France, and in Italy. The Jugo-Slavs, the Armenians, the Syrians and Lebanese, the Arabs, all the oppressed peoples, all the victims, long helpless or resigned, of great historic deeds of injustice, all the martyrs of the past, all the outraged consciences, all the strangled liberties revived at the clash of our arms, and turned towards us, as their natural defenders. Thus the war gradually attained the fullness of its first significance, and became, in the fullest sense of the term, a crusade of humanity for Right; and if anything can console us in part at least, for the losses we have suffered, it is assuredly the thought that our victory is also the victory of Right.

This victory is complete, for the enemy only asked for the armistice to escape from an irretrievable military disaster. In the interest of justice and peace it now rests with you to reap from this victory its full fruits in order to carry out this immense task. You have decided to admit, at first, only the Allied or associated Powers, and, in so far as their interests are involved in the debates, the nations which remained neutral. You have thought that the terms of peace ought to be settled among ourselves before they are communicated to those against whom we have together fought the good fight. The solidarity which has united us during the war and has enabled us to win military success ought to remain unimpaired during the negotiations for, and after the signing of, the Treaty.

It is not only governments, but free peoples, who are represented here. Through the test of danger they have learned to know and help one another. They want their intimacy of yesterday to assume the peace of to-morrow. Vainly would our enemies seek to divide us. If they have not yet renounced their customary maneuvers, they will soon find that they are meeting to-day, as during the hostilities, a homogeneous block which nothing will be able to disintegrate. Even before the armistice you placed that necessary unity under the standard of the lofty moral and political truths of which President Wilson has nobly made himself the interpreter.

The Meaning of Justice

And in the light of those truths you intend to accomplish your mission. You will, therefore, seek nothing but justice, "justice that has no favorites," justice in territorial problems, justice in financial problems, justice in economic problems. But justice is not inert, it does not submit to injustice. What it demands first, when it has been violated, are restitution and reparation for the people and individuals who have been despoiled or maltreated. In formulating this lawful claim, it obeys neither hatred nor an instinctive or thoughtless desire for reprisals. It pursues a twofold object—to render to each his due, and not to encourage crime through leaving it unpunished. What justice also demands, inspired by the same feeling, is the punishment of the guilty and effective guaranties against an active return of the spirit by which they were tempted; and it is logical to demand that these guaranties should be given, above all, to the nations that have been, and might again be most exposed to aggressions or threats, to those who have many times stood in danger of being submerged by the periodic tide of the same invasions.

What justice banishes is the dream of conquest and imperialism, contempt for national will, the arbitrary exchange of provinces between states as though peoples were but articles of furniture or pawns in a game. The time is no more when diplomatists could meet to redraw with authority the map of the empires on the corner of the table. If you are to remake the map of the world it is in the name of the peoples, and on condition that you shall faithfully interpret their thoughts, and respect the right of nations, small and great, to dispose of themselves, and to reconcile it with the right, equally sacred, of ethical and religious minorities—a formidable task, which science and history, your two advisers, will contribute to illumine and facilitate.

Establishing a New Order

You will naturally strive to secure the material and moral means of subsistence for all those peoples who are constituted or reconstituted into states; for those who wish to unite themselves to their neighbors; for those who divide themselves into separate units; for those who reorganize themselves according to their regained traditions; and, lastly, for all those whose freedom you already sanction or are about to sanction. You will not call them into existence only to sentence them to death immediately. You would like your work in this, as in all other matters, to be fruitful and lasting.

While thus introducing into the world as much harmony as possible, you will, in conformity with the fourteenth of the propositions unanimously adopted by the Great Allied Powers, establish a general League of Nations, which will be a supreme guaranty against any fresh assaults upon the right of peoples. You do not intend this International Association to be directed against anybody in future. It will not of set purpose shut out anybody, but, having been organized by the nations that have sacrificed themselves in defense of Right, it will receive from them its statutes and fundamental rules. It will lay down conditions to which its present or future adherents will submit, and, as it is to have for its essential aim to prevent, as far as possible, the renewal of wars, it will, above all, seek to gain respect for the peace which you will have established, and will find it the less difficult to maintain in proportion as this peace will in itself imply greater realities of justice and safer guaranties of stability.

By establishing this new order of things you will meet the aspiration of humanity, which, after the frightful convulsions of these bloodstained years, ardently wishes to feel itself protected by a union of free peoples against the ever-possible revivals of primitive savagery. An immortal glory will attach to the names of the nations and the men who have desired to coöperate in this grand work in faith and brotherhood, and who have taken pains to eliminate from the future peace causes of disturbance and instability.

This very day forty-eight years ago, on January 18, 1871, the German Empire was proclaimed by an army of invasion in the Château at Versailles. It was consecrated by the theft of two French provinces; it was thus vitiated from its origin and by the fault of the founders; born in injustice, it has ended in opprobrium. You are assembled in order to repair the evil that it has done and to prevent a recurrence of it. You hold in your hands the future of the world. I leave you, gentlemen, to your grave deliberations, and I declare the Conference of Paris open.

An Explanation
of the League
# of Nations

William Howard Taft

William Howard Taft, a lifelong American statesman, was elected the twenty-seventh president of the United States, serving from 1909 to 1913. Among his many other government positions, Taft was president of the League to Enforce Peace upon the conclusion of World War I. He was also an early and active advocate of ratification of the Treaty of Versailles at the end of the war.

One of the key provisions in the Treaty of Versailles was the establishment of a league of nations. This idea for an international organization for peace and arbitration came from President Woodrow Wilson. American involvement in the league, however, was a controversial matter long before the conclusion of the Paris Peace Conference. Taft's speech, delivered in the Metropolitan Opera House in New York on March 4, 1919, is an explanation of the proposed League of Nations. He offers an analysis of the articles of the League of Nations so that the American public will understand the nature and purpose of this governing body. Taft also addresses the criticisms that have been made about the proposed league, and he insists that American involvement in the organization is the only way to ensure international peace.

William Howard Taft, address at the Metropolitan Opera House, New York, March 4, 1919.

We are here to-night in the sight of a League of Peace, of what I have ever regarded as the "Promised Land." Such a war as the last is a hideous blot on our Christian civilization. The inconsistency is as foul as was slavery under the Declaration of Independence. If Christian nations cannot now be brought into a united effort to suppress a recurrence of such a contest it will be a shame to modern society.

Reduction of Armament

During my administration I attempted to secure treaties of universal arbitration between this country and France and England, by which all issues depending for their settlement upon legal principles were to be submitted to an international court for final decision. These treaties were emasculated by the Senate, yielding to the spirit which proceeds, unconsciously doubtless, but truly, from the conviction that the only thing that will secure to a nation the justice it wishes to secure is force; that agreements between nations to settle controversies justly and peaceably should never be given any weight in national policy; that in dealings between civilized nations we must assume that each nation is conspiring to deprive us of our independence and our prosperity; that there is no impartial tribunal to which we can entrust the decision of any question vitally affecting our interests or our honor, and that we can afford to make no agreement from which we may not immediately withdraw, and whose temporary operation to our detriment may not be expressly a ground for ending it. This is the doctrine of despair. It leads necessarily to the conclusion that our only recourse to avoid war is competitive armament, with its dreadful burdens and its constant temptation to the war it seeks to avoid.

The first important covenant with reference to peace and war in the Constitution of the League is that looking to a reduction of armament by all nations. The Executive Council, consisting of representatives of the United States, the British Empire, France, Italy, Japan, and of four other nations to be selected by the body of delegates, is to consider how much the armaments of the nations should be reduced, having regard to the safety of each of the nations and their obligations under the League. Having reached a conclusion as to the proportionate limits of each nation's armament, it submits its conclusion to each nation, which may or may not agree to the limit thus recommended; but when an agreement is reached it covenants to keep within that limit until, by application to the Executive Council, the limit may be raised. In other words, each nation agrees to its own limitation. Having so agreed it must keep within it.

The importance of providing for a reduction of armament every one recognizes. It is affirmed in the newly proposed Senate resolution. Can we not trust our Congress to fix a limitation safe for the country and to stick to it? If we can't, no country can. Yet all the rest are anxious to do this and they are far more exposed than we.

The character of this obligation is affected by the time during which the covenants of the League remain binding. There is no stipulation as to how long this is. In my judgment there should be a period of ten years or a permission for any member of the League to withdraw from the covenant by giving a reasonable notice of one or two years of its intention to do so.

International Arbitration to Settle Differences

The members of the League and the non-members are required, the former by their covenant, the latter by an enforced obligation, to submit all differences between them not capable of being settled by negotiation to arbitration before a tribunal composed as the parties may agree. They are required to covenant to abide the award. Should either party deem the question one not proper for arbitration then it is to be taken up by the Executive Council of the League. The Executive Council mediates between the parties and secures a voluntary settlement of the question if possible; if it fails, it makes a report. If the report is unanimous, the Executive Council is to recommend what shall be done to carry into effect its recommendation. If there is a dissenting vote, then the majority report is published, and the minority report, if desired, and no further action is taken. If either party of the Executive Council itself desires, the mediating function is to be discharged by the body of delegates in which every member of the League has one vote. There is no direction as to what shall be done with reference to the recommendation of proper measures to be taken, and the whole matter is then left for such further action as the members of the League agree upon. There is no covenant by the defeated party that it will comply with the unanimous report of the Executive Council or the Body of the League. . . .

These articles compelling submission of differences either to arbitration or mediation are not complete machinery for settlement by peaceable means of all issues arising between nations. But they are a substantial step forward. They are an unambitious plan to settle as many questions as possible by arbitration or mediation. They illustrate the spirit of those who drafted this covenant and their sensible desire not to attempt more till after actual experience.

The next covenant is that the nations shall not begin war until three months after the arbitration award or the recommendation of compromise, and not then if the defendant nation against whom the award or recommendation has been made shall comply with it. This is the great restraint of war imposed by the covenant upon members of the League and non-members. It is said that this would prevent our resistance to a border raid of Mexico or self-defense against any invasion. This is most extreme construction. If a nation refuses submission at all, as it does when it begins an attack, the nation attacked is released instanter from its obligation to submit and is restored to the complete power of self-defense. Had this objection not been raised in the Senate one would not have deemed it necessary to answer so unwarranted a suggestion.

If the defendant nation does not comply with the award or unanimous report, then the plaintiff nation can begin war and carry out such complete remedy as the circumstances enable it to do. But if the defendant nation does comply with the award or unanimous report, then the plaintiff nation must be content with such compliance. It runs the risk of not getting all it thought it ought to have or might have by war, but as it is asking affirmative relief it must be seeking some less vital interest than its political independence or territorial integrity, and the limitation is not one which can be dangerous to its sovereignty.

War Against One Is War Against All

The third covenant, the penalizing covenant, is that if a nation begins war, in violation of its covenant, then *ipso facto* ["by the fact itself"] that it is an act of war against every member of the League, and the members of the League are required definitely and distinctly to levy a boycott on the covenant-breaking nation and to cut off from it all commercial, trade, financial, personal, and official relations between them and their citizens and it and its citizens. Indeed, the boycott is compound or secondary, in that it is directed against any non-members of the League continuing to deal with the outlaw nation. This is an obligation operative at once on each member of the League. With us the Executive Council would report the violation of the covenant to the President and that would be reported to Congress, and Congress would then, by reason of the covenant of the League, be under an honorable legal and moral obligation to levy an embargo and prevent all intercourse of every kind between this nation and the covenant-breaking nation.

The extent of this penalty and its heavy withering effect when the hostile action includes all members of the League, as well as non-members, may be easily appreciated. The prospect of such an isolation would be likely to frighten any member of the League from a reckless violation of its covenant to begin war. It is inconceivable that any small nation, dependent as it must be on larger nations for its trade and sustenance, indeed for its food and raw material, would for a moment court such a destructive ostracism as this would be. . . .

Objections in the Senate

A proposed resolution in the Senate recites that the Constitution of the League of Nations in the form now proposed should not be accepted by the United States, although the sense of the Senate is that the nations of the world should unite to promote peace and general disarmament. The resolution further recites that the negotiations on the part of the United States should immediately be directed to the utmost expedition of the urgent business of negotiating peace terms with Germany satisfactory to the United States and the nations with whom the United States is associated in the war against the German government, and that the proposal for a League of Nations to insure the permanent peace of the world should then be taken up for careful and serious consideration. It is said that this resolution will be supported by thirty-seven members of the new Senate, and thus defeat the confirmation of any treaty which includes the present proposed covenant of Paris.

The President of the United States is the authority under the Federal Constitution which initiates the form of treaties and which at the outset determines what subject matter they shall include. Therefore, if it shall seem to the President of the United States and to those acting with him and with similar authority for other nations that a treaty of peace cannot be concluded except with a covenant providing for a League of Nations in substance like that now proposed as a condition precedent to the proper operation and effectiveness of the treaty itself, it will be the duty of the President and his fellow delegates to the conference to insert such a covenant in the treaty. If, accordingly, such a covenant shall be incorporated in a treaty of peace, signed by the representatives of the Powers and shall be brought back by the President and submitted by him to the Senate, the question which will address itself to the proponents of this Senate resolution will be not whether they would prefer to consider a League of Nations after the treaty of peace but whether they will feel justified in defeating or postponing a treaty because it contains a constitution of a League of Nations deemed by the President necessary to the kind of peace which all seek.

The Covenant Is the Key to Peace

The covenant of Paris, which is now a covenant only between the nations at war with Germany, including the seven nations who actually won the war, is essential to an effective treaty of peace to accomplish the purposes of the war; for the purposes of the war were to defeat militarism, to make the world safe for democracy, and to secure permanent peace.

Under the informal agreement between the nations who won this war, outlined in the President's message of January 8, 1918, as qualified by the Entente Allies before the armistice, we are to create and recognize as independent states four nations forming a bulwark between Germany and Russia to prevent future intrigues by Germany to secure control of Russia. In the process we are to carve these new nations out of the great autocracies, Russia, Germany, and Austria. We are to give German and Austrian Poland to the republic of Poland, to set up the Czecho-Slovak state of ten million inhabitants between Germany and Austria-Hungary, as well as the Jugoslav state carved out of Austria, and Hungary in the south. We are to fix new boundaries in the Balkans, with Rumania enlarged by Transylvania and Bessarabia, and to make an internationalized government at Constantinople, keeping ward over the passage between the Black Sea and the Ægean, and to establish autonomous dominions in Palestine, Syria, Armenia, and Mesopotamia. This plan for the peace and the reasons for it were set out with great force and vision by Senator [Henry Cabot] Lodge in a speech last January. The chief purpose of the plan is to take away the possibility that Germany shall ever again conceive and carry toward accomplishment her dream of the control of Russia and of a Middle European and Asiatic Empire, reaching from Hamburg to the Persian Gulf.

The plan thus requires not only the establishment but the continued maintenance of seven new republics in Europe and several autonomies in Asia Minor. We are to create twenty nations instead of four; and we are to carve the new ones out of the old ones. The peoples of the new republics will not have had experience in self-government. They are the children of the League of Nations, as Cuba has been our child. The League must continue to be a guardian of their internal stability, if they are to serve their purpose. Their natural resentment for past oppression against the neighboring countries out of which they have been carved and the corresponding hatred of them by the defeated peoples of those countries will at once produce controversies innumerable over the interpretation of the treaty and its application. Even the new countries as between themselves, with their natural lack of self-restraint and their indefinite ideas of their powers, have already come into forced conflict.

Unless there be some means for authoritatively interpreting the treaty and applying it, and unless the power of the League be behind it to give effect to such interpretation and application, the treaty instead of producing peace will produce a state of continued war. . . .

Withdrawal of the United States Will Weaken the League

If it be said that the European nations should unite in a league to maintain these independent states and settle the difficulties arising between them and the older states in the sphere of war, as well as to resist Bolshevism, it is sufficient to say that the withdrawal of the United States from the League of Nations will weaken it immeasurably. The disinterestedness of the United States, its position as the greatest Power in the world in view of its people and their intelligence and adaptability, its enormous natural resources, and its potential military power, demonstrated on the fields of France and Belgium, make its membership in the League indispensable. The confidence of the world in its disinterestedness and in its pure democracy will enormously enhance the prestige and power of the League's earnest desire for peace with justice.

For the United States to withdraw would make a league of other nations nothing but a return to the system of alliances and the balance of power with a certain speedy recurrence of war, in which the United States would be as certainly involved as it was in this war. The new inventions for the destruction of men and peoples would finally result in world suicide, while in the interval there would be a story of progressive competition in armaments, with all their heavy burdens upon the peoples of the nations, already oppressed almost to the point of exhaustion. With such a prospect and to avoid such results the United States should not hesitate to take its place with the other responsible nations of the world and make the light concessions and assume the light burdens involved in membership in the League.

No critic of the League has offered a single constructive suggestion to meet the crisis that I have thus summarily touched upon. The resolution of the Senate does not suggest or refer in any way to machinery by which the function of the League of Nations in steadying Europe and the maintaining of the peace agreed upon in the Peace Treaty shall be secured. Well may the President, therefore, decline to comply with the suggestions of the proposed resolution. Well may he say when he returns with the treaty, of which the covenant shall be a most important and indispensable part, "If you would postpone peace, if you would defeat it, you can refuse to ratify the Treaty. Amend it by striking out the covenant and you will have confusion worse confounded, with the objects of the war unattained and sacrificed and Europe and the world in dangerous chaos."

Objection is made that the covenant of the League is a departure from the traditional policy of the United States following the advice of Washington in avoiding entangling alliances with European nations. The European war into which we were drawn demonstrates that the policy is no longer possible for the United States. It has ceased to be a struggling nation. It has been made a close neighbor of Great Britain and France and Italy and of all nations of Europe, and is in such intimate trade relations that in a general European war it never can be a neutral again. It tried to be in this war and failed. Whatever nation secures the control of the seas will make the United States its ally, no matter how formal and careful its neutrality, because it will be the sole customer of the United States in food, raw material, and war necessities. Modern war is carried on in the mines and the workshops and on the farm, as well as in the trenches. The former are indispensable to the work in the latter. Hence the United States will certainly be drawn in, and hence its interests are inevitably involved in the preservation of European peace. These conditions and circumstances are so different from those in Washington's day, and are so unlike anything which we could have anticipated, that no words of his having relation to selfish offensive and defensive alliances such as he described in favor of one nation and against another should be given any application to the present international status. . . .

Look Forward

To suppose that the conditions in America and in Europe can be maintained absolutely separate, with the great trade relations between North America and Europe, is to look backward, not forward. It does not face existing conditions.

The European nations desire our entrance into this League, not that they may control America but to secure our aid in controlling Europe, and I venture to think that they would be relieved if the primary duty of keeping peace and policing this western hemisphere were relegated to us and our western colleagues. I object, however, to such a reservation as was contained in the Hague Conference [1907] against entangling alliances, because the recommendation was framed before this war and contained provisions as to the so-called policy against entangling alliances that are inconsistent with the present needs of this nation and of the rest of the world if a peaceful future is to be secured to both. I would favor, however, a recognition of the Monroe Doctrine[1] by specific words in the covenant, and with a further provision that the settlement of purely American questions should be remitted primarily to the American nations, with machinery like that of the present League, and that European nations should not intervene unless requested to do so by the American nations. . . .

Sovereignty Is Linked to Liberty

Finally, it is objected that we have no right to agree to arbitrate issues. It is said that we might by arbitration lose our territorial integrity or our political independence. This is a stretch of imagination by the distinguished Senator who made it, at which we marvel. In the face of Article X, which is an understanding to respect the territorial integrity and political independence of every member of the League, how could a board of arbitration possibly reach such a result?

1. Declared in 1823 by U.S. president James Monroe, the Monroe Doctrine called for a halt of European colonization on the American continents.

More than that, we do not have to arbitrate. If we do not care to arbitrate, we can throw the matter into mediation and conciliation, and we do not covenant to obey the recommendation of compromise by the conciliating body. We have been arbitrating questions for one hundred years.

We have stipulated in treaties to arbitrate classes of questions long before the questions arise. How would we arbitrate under this treaty? The form of the issue to be arbitrated would have to be formulated by our treaty-making power—the President and the Senate of the United States. The award would have to be performed by that branch of the government which executes awards, generally the Congress of the United States. If it involved payment of money, Congress would have to appropriate it. If it involved limitation of armament, Congress would have to limit it. If it involved any duty within the legislative power of Congress under the Constitution, Congress would have to perform it. If Congress sees fit to comply with the report of the compromise by the conciliating body, Congress will have to make such compliance.

The covenant takes away the sovereignty of the United States only as any contract curtails the freedom of action of an individual which he has voluntarily surrendered for the purpose of the contract and to obtain the benefit of it. The covenant creates no super-sovereignty. It merely creates contract obligations. It binds nations to stand together to secure compliance with those obligations. That is all. This is no different from a contract that we make with one nation. If we enter into an important contract with another nation to pay money or to do other things of vital interest to that nation and we break it, then we expose ourselves to the just effort of that nation by force of arms to attempt to compel us to comply with our obligations. This covenant of all the nations is only a limited and loose union of the compelling powers of many nations to do the same thing. The assertion that we are giving up our sovereignty carries us logically and necessarily to the absurd result that we cannot make a contract to do anything with another nation because it limits our freedom of action as a sovereign.

Sovereignty is freedom of action and nations. It is exactly analogous to the liberty of the individual regulated by law.

The sovereignty that we should insist upon, and the only sovereignty we have a right to insist upon, is a sovereignty regulated by international law, international morality, and international justice, a sovereignty enjoining the sacred rights which sovereignties of other nations may enjoy, a sovereignty consistent with the enjoyment of the same sovereignty of other nations. It is a sovereignty limited by the law of nations and limited by the obligation of contracts fully and freely entered into in respect to matters which are usually the subjects of contracts between nations.

The President Recommends the League

The President [Wilson] is now returning to Europe. As the representative of this nation in the conference he has joined in recommending in this proposed covenant a League of Nations for consideration and adoption by the conference. He has, meantime, returned home to discharge other executive duties, and it has given him an opportunity to note a discussion of the League in the Senate of the United States and elsewhere. Some speeches, notably that of Senator Lodge, have been useful in taking up the League, article by article, criticizing its language, and expressing doubt either as to its meaning or as to its wisdom.

He will differ, as many others will differ, from Senator Lodge in respect to many of the criticisms, but he will find many useful suggestions in the constructive part of the speech which he will be able to present to his colleagues in the conference. They will be especially valuable in revising the form of the covenant and making reservations to which his colleagues in the conference may readily consent, where Senator Lodge or the other critics have misunderstood the purpose and meaning of the words used.

This covenant should be in the treaty of peace. It is indispensable in ending the war, if the war is to accomplish the declared purpose of this nation and the world in that war, and if it is to work the promised benefit to mankind. We know the President believes this and will insist upon it. Our profound sympathy in his purpose and our prayers for his success should go with him in his great mission.

Justice Is What Germany Shall Have

Georges Clemenceau

Georges Clemenceau was a journalist and prominent French statesman. He served in the Chamber of Deputies for many years and became premier of France twice, from 1906 to 1909 and again from 1917 to 1920. He also served as minister of war during his tenure. When the Paris Peace Conference commenced in January 1919, President Woodrow Wilson successfully nominated Clemenceau as president of the conference. During the peace negotiations, however, Clemenceau often disagreed with Wilson. He considered the American president too idealistic.

Clemenceau made a number of speeches during the six-month peace conference. He gave the following address on June 16, 1919. He assigns full responsibility and guilt for the war to Germany and criticizes German tactics and conduct throughout the war. In Clemenceau's view, Germany is guilty of a crime against humanity. He strongly states that justice must be meted out through reparations and other measures. Clemenceau was not satisfied with the Versailles treaty, though, and ultimately maintained that its terms were too lenient.

I n the view of the Allied and Associated Powers the war which began on August 1st, 1914, was the greatest crime against humanity and the freedom of peoples that any nation, calling itself civilised, has ever consciously committed. For many years the rulers of Germany, true to the Prussian

Georges Clemenceau, address before the Paris Peace Conference, June 16, 1919.

tradition, strove for a position of dominance in Europe. They were not satisfied with that growing prosperity and influence to which Germany was entitled, and which all other nations were willing to accord her, in the society of free and equal peoples. They required that they should be able to dictate and tyrannise to a subservient Europe, as they dictated and tyrannised over a subservient Germany. Germany's responsibility, however, is not confined to having planned and started the war. She is no less responsible for the savage and inhuman manner in which it was conducted.

Germany's Crime

Though Germany was herself a guarantor of Belgium, the rulers of Germany violated, after a solemn promise to respect it, the neutrality of this unoffending people. Not content with this, they deliberately carried out a series of promiscuous shootings and burnings with the sole object of terrifying the inhabitants into submission by the very frightfulness of their action. They were the first to use poisonous gas, notwithstanding the appalling suffering it entailed. They began the bombing and long distance shelling of towns for no military object, but solely for the purpose of reducing the morale of their opponents by striking at their women and children. They commenced the submarine campaign with its piratical challenge to international law, and its destruction of great numbers of innocent passengers and sailors, in mid ocean, far from succour, at the mercy of the winds and the waves, and the yet more ruthless submarine crews. They drove thousands of men and women and children with brutal savagery into slavery in foreign lands. They allowed barbarities to be practised against their prisoners of war from which the most uncivilised people would have recoiled.

The conduct of Germany is almost unexampled [without precedent] in human history. The terrible responsibility which lies at her doors can be seen in the fact that not less than seven million dead lie buried in Europe, while more than twenty million others carry upon them the evidence of wounds and sufferings, because Germany saw fit to gratify her lust for tyranny by resort to war.

The Allied and Associated Powers believe that they will be false to those who have given their all to save the freedom of the world if they consent to treat this war on any other basis than as a crime against humanity.

Justice, therefore, is the only possible basis for the settlement of the accounts of this terrible war. Justice is what the German Delegation asks for and says that Germany had been promised. Justice is what Germany shall have. But it must be justice for all. There must be justice for the dead and wounded and for those who have been orphaned and bereaved that Europe might be freed from Prussian despotism. There must be justice for the peoples who now stagger under war debts which exceed £30,000,000,000 that liberty might be saved. There must be justice for those millions whose homes and land, ships and property German savagery has spoliated [to strip or rob by force] and destroyed.

That is why the Allied and Associated Powers have insisted as a cardinal feature of the Treaty that Germany must undertake to make reparation to the very uttermost of her power; for reparation for wrongs inflicted is of the essence of justice. That is why they insist that those individuals who are most clearly responsible for German aggression and for those acts of barbarism and inhumanity which have disgraced the German conduct of the war, must be handed over to a justice which has not been meted out to them at home. That, too, is why Germany must submit for a few years to certain special disabilities and arrangements. Germany has ruined the industries, the mines and the machinery of neighbouring countries, not during battle, but with the deliberate and calculated purpose of enabling her industries to seize their markets before their industries could recover from the devastation thus wantonly inflicted upon them. Germany has despoiled her neighbours of everything she could make use of or carry away. Germany has destroyed the shipping of all nations on the high sea, where there was no chance of rescue for their passengers and crews. It is only justice that restitution should be made and that these wronged peoples should be safeguarded for a time from the competition of a nation whose industries are intact and have even been fortified by machinery stolen from occupied territories.

GREAT
SPEECHES
IN
HISTORY

The Legacy
of the War

The United States Should Not Join the League of Nations

Henry Cabot Lodge

Germany's surrender and the Paris Peace Conference were based on President Woodrow Wilson's Fourteen Points, which he outlined in January 1918. Among these points, which were devised as goals for postwar peace, were national self-determination, freedom of the seas, and the renunciation of secret treaties. The most notable of the points was the provision for an international league of nations to maintain world order and arbitrate in disputes. The constitution for the League of Nations was incorporated into the Versailles treaty. However, there was heated congressional debate over U.S. entry into the league, and the United States never ratified the treaty or joined the league.

The most vocal opponent of the League of Nations was Republican senator Henry Cabot Lodge, who campaigned against U.S. membership. In a speech before Congress on August 12, 1919, Lodge raises objections to American participation in an international governing body. In his view, the United States should concentrate on its own affairs in the postwar period. He warns against idealism that may not be shared by all nations, and he argues for a realistic view of the world situation. Above all, Lodge is firm in his belief that America should work on maintaining its position as a strong, independent country, and that any participation in international politics would weaken the United States.

Henry Cabot Lodge, address to the United States Congress, August 12, 1919.

Mr. President:
The independence of the United States is not only more precious to ourselves but to the world than any single possession. Look at the United States today. We have made mistakes in the past. We have had shortcomings. We shall make mistakes in the future and fall short of our own best hopes. But none the less is there any country to-day on the face of the earth which can compare with this in ordered liberty, in peace, and in the largest freedom?

I feel that I can say this without being accused of undue boastfulness, for it is the simple fact, and in making this treaty and taking on these obligations all that we do is in a spirit of unselfishness and in a desire for the good of mankind. But it is well to remember that we are dealing with nations every one of which has a direct individual interest to serve, and there is grave danger in an unshared idealism.

Contrast the United States with any country on the face of the earth today and ask yourself whether the situation of the United States is not the best to be found. I will go as far as anyone in world service, but the first step to world service is the maintenance of the United States.

I have always loved one flag and I cannot share that devotion [with] a mongrel banner created for a League.

You may call me selfish if you will, conservative or reactionary, or use any other harsh adjective you see fit to apply, but an American I was born, an American I have remained all my life. I can never be anything else but an American, and I must think of the United States first, and when I think of the United States first in an arrangement like this I am thinking of what is best for the world, for if the United States fails, the best hopes of mankind fail with it.

I have never had but one allegiance—I cannot divide it now. I have loved but one flag and I cannot share that devotion and give affection to the mongrel banner invented for a league. Internationalism, illustrated by the Bolshevik and by the men to whom all countries are alike provided they can make money out of them, is to me repulsive.

National I must remain, and in that way I like all other Americans can render the amplest service to the world. The United States is the world's best hope, but if you fetter her in the interests and quarrels of other nations, if you tangle her in the intrigues of Europe, you will destroy her power for good and endanger her very existence. Leave her to march freely through the centuries to come as in the years that have gone.

Strong, generous, and confident, she has nobly served mankind. Beware how you trifle with your marvellous inheritance, this great land of ordered liberty, for if we stumble and fall freedom and civilization everywhere will go down in ruin.

We are told that we shall 'break the heart of the world' if we do not take this league just as it stands. I fear that the hearts of the vast majority of mankind would beat on strongly and steadily and without any quickening if the league were to perish altogether. If it should be effectively and beneficently changed the people who would lie awake in sorrow for a single night could be easily gathered in one not very large room but those who would draw a long breath of relief would reach to millions.

We hear much of visions and I trust we shall continue to have visions and dream dreams of a fairer future for the race. But visions are one thing and visionaries are another, and the mechanical appliances of the rhetorician designed to give a picture of a present which does not exist and of a future which no man can predict are as unreal and short-lived as the steam or canvas clouds, the angels suspended on wires and the artificial lights of the stage.

They pass with the moment of effect and are shabby and tawdry in the daylight. Let us at least be real. Washington's entire honesty of mind and his fearless look into the face of all facts are qualities which can never go out of fashion and which we should all do well to imitate.

Our Country Has Her Own Problems

Ideals have been thrust upon us as an argument for the league until the healthy mind which rejects can't revolt from them. Are ideals confined to this deformed experiment upon a noble purpose, tainted, as it is, with bargains and tied to a peace treaty which might have been disposed of long ago to the great benefit of the world if it had not been compelled to carry this rider on its back? 'Post equitem sedet ara cura'[1] Horace[2] tells us, but no blacker care ever sat behind any rider than we shall find in this covenant of doubtful and disputed interpretation as it now perches upon the treaty of peace.

No doubt many excellent and patriotic people see a coming fulfilment of noble ideals in the words 'league for peace.' We all respect and share these aspirations and desires, but some of us see no hope, but rather defeat, for them in this murky covenant. For we, too, have our ideals, even if we differ from those who have tried to establish a monopoly of idealism.

Our first ideal is our country, and we see her in the future, as in the past, giving service to all her people and to the world. Our ideal of the future is that she should continue to render that service of her own free will. She has great problems of her own to solve, very grim and perilous problems, and a right solution, if we can attain to it, would largely benefit mankind.

We would have our country strong to resist a peril from the West, as she has flung back the German menace from the East. We would not have our politics distracted and embittered by the dissensions of other lands. We would not have our country's vigour exhausted or her moral force abated, by everlasting meddling and muddling in every quarrel, great and small, which afflicts the world.

Our ideal is to make her ever stronger and better and finer, because in that way alone, as we believe, can she be of the greatest service to the world's peace and to the welfare of mankind.

---

1. "Behind the rider sits dark care"   2. a famous Roman poet who lived from 65 to 8 B.C.

Senators Should Support the League of Nations

Gilbert M. Hitchcock

Gilbert M. Hitchcock was a supporter of President Woodrow Wilson and a vocal advocate for U.S. membership in the League of Nations. This speech by Hitchcock, a Democrat and the Senate minority leader, is in response to his anti-league counterpart, Republican and Senate majority leader Henry Cabot Lodge. Hitchcock was President Wilson's liaison throughout the league struggle, and this address represents his efforts to persuade his colleagues that the world has entered a new age of internationalism. Hitchcock expresses his belief that governments should end war and that the chief aim of government should be the preservation of peace. His speech, delivered on the Senate floor on September 3, 1919, is also a pointed commentary on the anti-league senators. He suggests that those senators in opposition to the League of Nations fail to understand that the world of conquering empires is gone and that the only way to ensure peace is to create a league of nations to govern with justice and reason.

The trouble with Senators who oppose the League of Nations is that they are thinking of the days that are gone and gone forever. The conquering empires of the world have been wiped out. The fall of Russia and Germany

Gilbert M. Hitchcock, address to the United States Senate, September 3, 1919.

and Austria-Hungary removed from the world the last representatives of the conquering spirit and of autocratic power. The world is now democratic. Senators should cease to turn their eyes to the past and should turn them to the future, and see what we have before us.

Governments Should End War

The spirit of democracy has come into its own. We have come into a new world. We are about to organize the democracies of the earth to establish law and order among the nations. And we can do it now for the first time in the history of the world. We need take in no despots. We need take into consideration no conquering empire. That day has gone, and we have come into a new era. The senators should realize it. Let them grasp the fact that the spirit of the age is to end conquest. That the spirit of the age is to have the people rule. That the spirit of the age is that governments shall be content to serve their own people and not to despoil others. Let them see the New World as it is, and the new spirit which inspires it. Let them appreciate the fact that humanity is not willing to sacrifice itself further, that men and women demand of their government that as the fruit of this terrible war an agreement shall be entered into for the preservation of world peace in the future. If senators will turn from the past towards the future, they will behold a new heaven and a new earth, not a millennium perhaps, but a world in which the affairs of nations are to be administered in justice and reason and humanity. A world in which the chief affair of government shall be peace and development and progress. A world in which man shall attain its highest destiny and happiness. This was impossible in the days of tyrants and autocrats and conquerors, but it is possible in the new age of liberty, statesmanship, and philanthropy.

The late war cost seven million lives, and millions more of cripples. It has destroyed hundreds of towns, it has widowed millions of wives, it has brought in its train the inevitable consequences of war, pestilence, and famine. One of the war diseases alone has cost this country over three hundred thousand lives of the civilian population. It has let loose and inflamed the passions and lusts of man, and crushed and humiliated millions of women. Massacre, torture, and assassinations have accompanied it. Law and order have been overthrown. Bolshevism and anarchy have been profligated. The confidence of men in government has been shaken. It will never be restored until governments devise some way to end war. The League of Nations is that way.

Wilson's Vision for a League of Nations

Woodrow Wilson

This speech by U.S. president Woodrow Wilson responds to the criticisms made by Senator Henry Cabot Lodge and other congressional opponents of the League of Nations. The league was envisioned as an international organization designed to maintain peace and justice throughout the world. Although Wilson was confident in the league's potential to protect people everywhere, many Americans were concerned about the extent to which the United States would be involved in the disputes of other nations. The contention surrounding the league proposal prompted Wilson to embark on a speaking tour of the United States. For many months he spoke to crowds, defending the League of Nations and emphasizing the importance of U.S. membership. He believed that the role of the United States was key to lasting world peace.

In this public address, delivered in Pueblo, Colorado, on September 25, 1919, Wilson describes the terms of the Versailles peace settlement and delineates the structure and function of the League of Nations. Wilson clarifies the obligations the United States would undertake as a member of the league. He also highlights the ideals of liberty, justice, and peace inherent to the international organization. The pro-league speech in Pueblo was to be Wilson's last. After delivering the speech, Wilson collapsed; a week later he suffered a stroke. The stroke left him incapacitated for the rest of his term. He continued to oppose severe restrictions to the league, even from his sickbed. The final re-

Woodrow Wilson, address in Pueblo, Colorado, September 25, 1919.

fusal to ratify the Treaty of Versailles and join the League of Nations was confirmed in a Senate vote on March 19, 1920. The treaty fell seven votes short of ratification.

Mr. Chairman and fellow countrymen: It is with a great deal of genuine pleasure that I find myself in Pueblo, and I feel it a compliment in this beautiful hall. One of the advantages of this hall, as I look about, is that you are not too far away from me, because there is nothing so reassuring to men who are trying to express the public sentiment as getting into real personal contact with their fellow citizens. I have gained a renewed impression as I have crossed the continent this time of the homogeneity of this great people to whom we belong. They come from many stocks, but they are all of one kind. They come from many origins, but they are all shot through with the same principles and desire the same righteous and honest things. I have received a more inspiring impression this time of the public opinion of the United States than it was ever my privilege to receive before.

The chief pleasure of my trip has been that it has nothing to do with my personal fortunes, that it has nothing to do with my personal reputation, that it has nothing to do with anything except great principles uttered by Americans of all sorts and of all parties which we are now trying to realize at this crisis of the affairs of the world. But there have been unpleasant impressions as well as pleasant impressions, my fellow citizens, as I have crossed the continent. I have perceived more and more that men have been busy creating an absolutely false impression of what the treaty of peace and the Covenant of the League of Nations contain and mean. I find, moreover, that there is an organized propaganda against the League of Nations and against the treaty proceeding from exactly the same sources that the organized propaganda proceeded from which threatened this country here and there with disloyalty, and I want to say—I cannot say too often—any man who carries a hyphen about with him carries a dagger that he is ready to plunge into the vitals of this Republic whenever he gets ready. If I can catch any man with a hyphen in this great contest I will know that I have got an enemy of the Republic. My fellow citizens, it is only certain bodies of foreign sympathies, certain bodies of sympathy with foreign nations that are organized against this great document which the American representatives have brought back from Paris. Therefore, in order to clear away the mists, in order to remove the impressions, in order to check the falsehoods that have clustered around this great subject, I want to tell you a few very simple things about the treaty and the covenant.

A People's Treaty

Do not think of this treaty of peace as merely a settlement with Germany. It is that. It is a very severe settlement with Germany, but there is not anything in it that she did not earn. Indeed, she earned more than she can ever be able to pay for, and the punishment exacted of her is not a punishment greater than she can bear, and it is absolutely necessary in order that no other nation may ever plot such a thing against humanity and civilization. But the treaty is so much more than that. It is not merely a settlement with Germany; it is a readjustment of those great injustices which underlie the whole structure of European and Asiatic society. This is only the first of several treaties. They are all constructed upon the same plan. The Austrian treaty follows the same lines. The treaty with Hungary follows the same lines. The treaty with Bulgaria follows the same lines. The treaty with Turkey, when it is formulated, will follow the same lines. What are those lines? They are based upon the purpose to see that every government dealt with in this great settlement is put in the hands of the people and taken out of the hands of coteries and of sovereigns who had no right to rule over the people. It is a people's treaty, that accomplishes by a great sweep of practical justice the liberation of men who never could have liberated themselves, and the power of the most powerful nations has been devoted not to their aggrandizement but to the liberation of people whom they could have put under their control if they had chosen to do so. Not one foot of territory is demanded by the conquerors, not one single item of submission to their authority is demanded by them. The men who sat around that table in Paris knew that the time had come when the people were no longer going to consent to live under masters, but were going to live the lives that they chose themselves, to live under such governments as they chose themselves to erect. That is the fundamental principle of this great settlement.

And we did not stop with that. We added a great international charter for the rights of labor. Reject this treaty, impair it, and this is the consequence of the laboring men of the world, that there is no international tribunal which can bring the moral judgments of the world to bear upon the great labor questions of the day. What we need to do with regard to the labor questions of the day, my fellow countrymen, is tilt them into the light, is to lift them out of the haze and distraction of passion, of hostility, out into the calm spaces where men look at things without passion. The more men you get into a great discussion is the more you exclude passion. Just as soon as the calm judgment of the world is directed upon the question of justice to labor, labor is going to have to forum such as it never was supplied with before, and men everywhere are going to see that the problem of labor is nothing more nor less than the problem of the elevation of humanity. We must see that all the questions which have disturbed the world, all the questions which have eaten into the confidence of men toward their governments, all the questions which have disturbed the processes of industry, shall be brought out where men of all points of view, men of all attitudes of mind, men of all kinds of experience, may contribute their part of the settlement of the great questions which we must settle and cannot ignore.

The League of Nations

At the front of this great treaty is put the Covenant of the League of Nations. It will also be at the front of the Austrian treaty and the Hungarian treaty and the Bulgarian treaty and the treaty with Turkey. Every one of them will contain the Covenant of the League of Nations, because you cannot work any of them without the Covenant of the League of Nations. Unless you get the united, concerted purpose and power of the great Governments of the world behind this settlement, it will fall down like a house of cards. There is only one power to put behind the liberation of mankind, and that is the power of mankind. It is the power of the united moral forces of the world, and in the Covenant of the League of Nations the moral forces of the world are mobilized. For what purpose? Reflect, my fellow citizens, that the membership of this great League is going to include all the great fighting nations of the world, as well as the weak ones. It is not for the present going to include Germany, but for the time being Germany is not a great fighting country. All the nations that have power that can be mobilized are going to be members of this League, including the United States. And what do they unite for? They enter into a solemn promise to one another that they will never use their power against one another for aggression; that they never will impair the territorial integrity of a neighbor; that they never will interfere with the political independence of a neighbor; that they will abide by the principle that great populations are entitled to determine their own destiny and that they will not interfere with that destiny; and that no matter what differences arise amongst them they will never resort to war without first having done one or other of two things—either submitted the matter of controversy to arbitration, in which case they agree to abide by the result without question, or submitted it to the consideration of the council of the League of Nations, laying before that council all the documents, all the facts, agreeing that the council can publish the documents and the facts to the whole world, agreeing that there shall be six months allowed for the mature consideration of those facts by the council, and agreeing that at the expiration of the six months, even if they are not then ready to accept the advice of the council with regard to the settlement of the dispute, they will still not go to war for another three months. In other words, they consent, no matter what happens, to submit every matter of difference between them to the judgment of mankind, and just so certainly as they do that, my fellow citizens, war will be in the far background, war will be pushed out of that foreground of terror in which it has kept the world for generation after generation, and men will know that there will be a calm time of deliberate counsel. The most dangerous thing for a bad cause is to expose it to the opinion of the world. The most certain way that you can prove that a man is mistaken is by letting all his neighbors know what he thinks, by letting all his neighbors discuss what he thinks, and if he is in the wrong you will notice that he will stay at home, he will not walk on the street. He will be afraid of the eyes of his neighbors. He will be afraid of their judgment of his character. He will know that his cause is lost unless he can sustain it by the arguments of right and of justice. The same law that applies to individuals applies to nations.

Organization of the League

But, you say, "We have heard that we might be at a disadvantage in the League of Nations." Well, whoever told you that either was deliberately falsifying or he had not read the Covenant of the League of Nations. I leave him the choice. I want to give you a very simple account of the organization of the League of Nations and let you judge for yourselves. It is a very simple organization. The power of the League, or rather the activities of the League, lie in two bodies. There is the council, which consists of one representative from each of the principal allied and associated powers—that is to say, the United States, Great Britain, France, Italy, and Japan, along with four other representatives of smaller powers chosen out of the general body of the membership of the League. The council is the source of every active policy of the League, and no active policy of the League can be adopted without a unanimous vote of the council. That is explicitly stated in the Covenant itself. Does it not evidently follow that the League of Nations can adopt no policy whatever without the consent of the United States? The affirmative vote of the representative of the United States is necessary in every case. Now, you have heard of six votes belonging to the British Empire. Those six votes are not in the council. They are in the assembly, and the interesting thing is that the assembly does not vote. I must qualify that statement a little, but essentially it is absolutely true. In every matter in which the assembly is given a voice, and there are only four or five, its vote does not count unless concurred in by the representatives of all the nations represented on the council, so that there is no validity to any vote of the assembly unless in that vote also the representative of the United States concurs. That one vote of the United States is as big as the six votes of the British Empire. I am not jealous for advantage, my fellow citizens, but I think that is a perfectly safe situation. There is no validity in a vote, either by the council or the assembly, in which we do not concur. So much for the statements about the six votes of the British Empire. . . .

Let us sweep aside all this language of jealousy. Let us be big enough to know the facts and to welcome the facts, because the facts are based upon the principle that America has always fought for, namely, the equality of self-governing peoples, whether they were big or little—not counting men, but counting rights, not counting representation, but counting the purpose of that representation. When you hear an opinion quoted you do not count the number of persons who hold it; you ask, "Who said that?" You weigh opinions, you do not count them, and the beauty of all democracies is that every voice can be heard, every voice can have its effect, every voice can contribute to the general judgment that is finally arrived at. That is the object of democracy. Let us accept what America has always fought for, and accept it with pride that America showed the way and made the proposal. I do not mean that America made the proposal in this particular instance; I mean that the principle was an American principle, proposed by America.

Well you come to the heart of the Covenant, my fellow citizens, you will find it in article ten, and I am very much interested to know that the other things have been blown away like bubbles. There is nothing in the other contentions with regard to the League of Nations, but there is something in article ten that you ought to realize and ought to accept or reject. Article ten is the heart of the whole matter. What is article ten? I never am certain that I can from memory give a literal repetition of its language, but I am sure that I can give an exact interpretation of its meaning. Article ten provides that every member of the league covenants to respect and preserve the territorial integrity and existing political inde-

pendence of every other member of the league as against external aggression. Not against internal disturbance. There
was not a man at that table who did not admit the sacredness
of the right of self determination, the sacredness of the right
of any body of people to say that they would not continue to
live under the Government they were then living under, and
under article eleven of the Covenant they are given a place to
say whether they will live under it or not. For following
article ten is article eleven, which makes it the right of any
member of the League at any time to call attention to anything, anywhere, that is likely to disturb the peace of the
world or the good understanding between nations upon
which the peace of the world depends. . . .

The Liberty of the World

I am dwelling upon these points, my fellow citizens, in spite
of the fact that I dare say to most of you they are perfectly
well known, because in order to meet the present situation
we have got to know what we are dealing with. We are not
dealing with the kind of document which this is represented
by some gentlemen to be; and inasmuch as we are dealing
with a document simon-pure in respect of the very principles
we have professed and lived up to, we have got to do one or
other of two things—we have got to adopt it or reject it.
There is no middle course. You cannot go in on a special-
privilege basis of your own. I take it that you are too proud
to ask to be exempted from responsibilities which the other
members of the League will carry. We go in upon equal terms
or we do not go in at all; and if we do not go in, my fellow
citizens, think of the tragedy of that result—the only sufficient guaranty to the peace of the world withheld! Ourselves
drawn apart with that dangerous pride which means that we
shall be ready to take care of ourselves, and that means that
we shall maintain great standing armies and an irresistible
navy; that means we shall have the organization of a military
nation; that means we shall have a general staff, with the
kind of power that the general staff of Germany had; to mobilize this great manhood of the Nation when it pleases, all
the energy of our young men drawn into the thought and

preparation for war. What of our pledges to the men that lie dead in France? We said that they went over there not to prove the prowess of America or her readiness for another war but to see to it that there never was such a war again. It always seems to make it difficult for me to say anything, my fellow citizens, when I think of my clients in this case. My clients are the children; my clients are the next generation. They do not know what promises and bonds I undertook when I ordered the armies of the United States to the soil of France, but I know, and I intend to redeem my pledges to the children; they shall not be sent upon a similar errand.

Again and again, my fellow citizens, mothers who lost their sons in France have come to me and, taking my hand, have shed tears upon it not only, but they have added, "God bless you, Mr. President!" Why, my fellow citizens, should they pray God to bless me? I advised the Congress of the United States to create the situation that led to the death of their sons. I ordered their sons overseas. I consented to their sons being put in the most difficult parts of the battle line, where death was certain, as in the impenetrable difficulties of the forest of Argonne. Why should they weep upon my hand and call down the blessings of God upon me? Because they believe that their boys died for something that vastly transcends any of the immediate and palpable objects of the war. They believe and they rightly believe, that their sons saved the liberty of the world. They believe that wrapped up with the liberty of the world is the continuous protection of that liberty by the concerted powers of all civilized people. They believe that this sacrifice was made in order that other sons should not be called upon for a similar gift—the gift of life, the gift of all that died—and if we did not see this thing through if we fulfilled the dearest present wish of Germany and now dissociated ourselves from those alongside whom we fought in the world, would not something of the halo go away from the gun over the mantelpiece, or the sword? Would not the old uniform lose something of its significance? These men were crusaders. They were not going forth to prove the might of the United States. They were going forth to prove the might of justice and right, and all the world accepted them as crusaders, and their transcendent achievement has made all the world believe in America as it believes in no other nation organized in the modern world. There seem to me to stand between us and the rejection or qualification of this treaty the serried ranks of those boys in khaki, not only these boys who came home, but those dear ghosts that still deploy upon the fields of France.

My friends, on last Decoration day I went to a beautiful hillside near Paris, where was located the cemetery of Suresnes, a cemetery given over to the burial of the American dead. Behind me all the slopes was rank upon rank of living American soldiers, and lying before me upon the levels of the plain was rank upon rank of departed American soldiers. Right by the side of the stand where I spoke there was a little group of French women who had adopted those graves, had made themselves mothers of those dear ghosts by putting flowers every day upon those graves, taking them as their own sons, their own beloved, because they had died in the same cause—France was free and the world was free because America had come! I wish some men in public life who are now opposing the settlement for which these men died could visit such a spot as that. I wish that the thought that comes out of those graves could penetrate their consciousness. I wish that they could feel the moral obligation that rests upon us not to go back on those boys, but to see the thing through, to see it through to the end and make good their redemption of the world. For nothing less depends upon this decision, nothing less than liberation and salvation of the world.

Truth Will Lead Us

You will say, "Is the League an absolute guaranty against war?" No; I do not know any absolute guaranty against the errors of human judgment or the violence of human passions but I tell you this: With a cooling space of nine months for human passion, not much of it will keep hot. I had a couple of friends who were in the habit of losing their tempers, and when they lost their tempers they were in the habit of using very unparliamentary language. Some of their friends induced them to make a promise that they never would swear inside the town limits. When the impulse next came upon them, they took a street car to go out of town to swear, and by the time they got out of town they did not want to swear. They came back convinced that they were just what they were, a couple of unspeakable fools, and the habit of getting angry and of swearing suffered great inroads upon it by that experience. Now, illustrating the great by the small, that is true of the passions of nations. It is true of the passions of men however you combine them. Give them space to cool off. I ask you this: If it is not an absolute insurance against war, do you want no insurance at all? Do you want nothing? Do you want not only no probability that war will not recur, but the probability that it will recur? The arrangements of justice do not stand of themselves, my fellow citizens. The arrangements of this treaty are just, but they need the support of the combined power of the great nations of the world. And they will have that support. Now that the mists of this great question have cleared away, I believe that men will see the truth, eye to eye and face to face. There is one thing that the American people always rise to and extend their hand to, and that is the truth of justice and of liberty and of peace. We have accepted that truth and we are going to be led by it, and it is going to lead us, and through us the world, out into pastures of quietness and peace such as the world never dreamed of before.

America Should Avoid Future Foreign Wars

Warren G. Harding

Warren G. Harding, a Republican senator from Ohio, was elected president in 1920. An opponent of the League of Nations, Harding was in the Senate throughout the contested debate over the Versailles treaty. His campaign was a plea for a return to "normalcy"—a word he used to mean the normal state of affairs for America. His landslide win in the first postwar presidential election reflected the American reaction against Woodrow Wilson's international vision.

Harding's inaugural address, delivered on March 4, 1921, evaluates the postwar leadership position of the United States in world affairs and talks about the American democratic ideals of freedom and independence. Harding recognizes the weight and responsibility of the United States in the new world order but is also careful to distance the United States from direct, committed involvement in the international scene. Emphasizing the nation's self-reliance, Harding believes that America must focus on domestic concerns and economic progress in the aftermath of the war. Throughout the 1920s, though, the United States turned its political focus to domestic affairs rather than international issues, and it became characterized by isolationism.

Warren G. Harding, Inaugural Address, March 4, 1921.

M y Countrymen:
When one surveys the world about him after the great storm, noting the marks of destruction and yet rejoicing in the ruggedness of the things which withstood it, if he is an American he breathes the clarified atmosphere with a strange mingling of regret and new hope. We have seen a world passion spend its fury, but we contemplate our Republic unshaken, and hold our civilization secure. Liberty—liberty within the law—and civilization are inseparable, and though both were threatened we find them now secure; and there comes to Americans the profound assurance that our representative government is the highest expression and surest guaranty of both.

Standing in this presence, mindful of the solemnity of this occasion, feeling the emotions which no one may know until he senses the great weight of responsibility for himself, I must utter my belief in the divine inspiration of the founding fathers. Surely there must have been God's intent in the making of this new-world Republic. Ours is an organic law which had but one ambiguity, and we saw that effaced in a baptism of sacrifice and blood, with union maintained, the Nation supreme, and its concord inspiring. We have seen the world rivet its hopeful gaze on the great truths on which the founders wrought. We have seen civil, human, and religious liberty verified and glorified. In the beginning the Old World scoffed at our experiment; today our foundations of political and social belief stand unshaken, a precious inheritance to ourselves, an inspiring example of freedom and civilization to all mankind. Let us express renewed and strengthened devotion, in grateful reverence for the immortal beginning, and utter our confidence in the supreme fulfillment.

Careful Involvement in International Affairs

The recorded progress of our Republic, materially and spiritually, in itself proves the wisdom of the inherited policy of noninvolvement in Old World affairs. Confident of our ability to work out our own destiny, and jealously guarding our right to do so, we seek no part in directing the destinies of the

Old World. We do not mean to be entangled. We will accept no responsibility except as our own conscience and judgment, in each instance, may determine.

Our eyes never will be blind to a developing menace, our ears never deaf to the call of civilization. We recognize the new order in the world, with the closer contacts which progress has wrought. We sense the call of the human heart for fellowship, fraternity, and cooperation. We crave friendship and harbor no hate. But America, our America, the America built on the foundation laid by the inspired fathers, can be a party to no permanent military alliance. It can enter into no political commitments, nor assume any economic obligations which will subject our decisions to any other than our own authority.

I am sure our own people will not misunderstand, nor will the world misconstrue. We have no thought to impede the paths to closer relationship. We wish to promote understanding. We want to do our part in making offensive warfare so hateful that Governments and peoples who resort to it must prove the righteousness of their cause or stand as outlaws before the bar of civilization.

We are ready to associate ourselves with the nations of the world, great and small, for conference, for counsel; to seek the expressed views of world opinion; to recommend a way to approximate disarmament and relieve the crushing burdens of military and naval establishments. We elect to participate in suggesting plans for mediation, conciliation, and arbitration, and would gladly join in that expressed conscience of progress, which seeks to clarify and write the laws of international relationship, and establish a world court for the disposition of such justiciable questions as nations are agreed to submit thereto. In expressing aspirations, in seeking practical plans, in translating humanity's new concept of righteousness and justice and its hatred of war into recommended action we are ready most heartily to unite, but every commitment must be made in the exercise of our national sovereignty. Since freedom impelled, and independence inspired, and nationality exalted, a world supergovernment is contrary to everything we cherish and can have no sanction by our Republic. This is not selfishness, it is sanctity. It is not

aloofness, it is security. It is not suspicion of others, it is patriotic adherence to the things which made us what we are.

Today, better than ever before, we know the aspirations
of humankind, and share them. We have come to a new realization of our place in the world and a new appraisal of our
Nation by the world. The unselfishness of these United States
is a thing proven; our devotion to peace for ourselves and for
the world is well established; our concern for preserved civilization has had its impassioned and heroic expression. There
was no American failure to resist the attempted reversion of
civilization; there will be no failure today or tomorrow.

The Will of America

The success of our popular government rests wholly upon the
correct interpretation of the deliberate, intelligent, dependable popular will of America. In a deliberate questioning of
a suggested change of national policy, where internationality
was to supersede nationality, we turned to a referendum, to
the American people. There was ample discussion, and there
is a public mandate in manifest understanding.

America is ready to encourage, eager to initiate, anxious
to participate in any seemly program likely to lessen the probability of war, and promote that brotherhood of mankind
which must be God's highest conception of human relationship. Because we cherish ideals of justice and peace, because
we appraise international comity and helpful relationship no
less highly than any people of the world, we aspire to a high
place in the moral leadership of civilization, and we hold a
maintained America, the proven Republic, the unshaken tem-
ple of representative democracy, to be not only an inspiration
and example, but the highest agency of strengthening good
will and promoting accord on both continents.

Mankind needs a world-wide benediction of understanding. It is needed among individuals, among peoples, among
governments, and it will inaugurate an era of good feeling to
make the birth of a new order. In such understanding men
will strive confidently for the promotion of their better relationships and nations will promote the comities so essential
to peace.

We must understand that ties of trade bind nations in closest intimacy, and none may receive except as he gives. We have not strengthened ours in accordance with our resources or our genius, notably on our own continent, where a galaxy of Republics reflects the glory of new-world democracy, but in the new order of finance and trade we mean to promote enlarged activities and seek expanded confidence.

Perhaps we can make no more helpful contribution by example than prove a Republic's capacity to emerge from the wreckage of war. While the world's embittered travail did not leave us devastated lands nor desolated cities, left no gaping wounds, no breast with hate, it did involve us in the delirium of expenditure, in expanded currency and credits, in unbalanced industry, in unspeakable waste, and disturbed relationships. While it uncovered our portion of hateful selfishness at home, it also revealed the heart of America as sound and fearless, and beating in confidence unfailing.

"No Spirit of Revenge"

Amid it all we have riveted the gaze of all civilization to the unselfishness and the righteousness of representative democracy, where our freedom never has made offensive warfare, never has sought territorial aggrandizement through force, never has turned to the arbitrament of arms until reason has been exhausted. When the Governments of the earth shall have established a freedom like our own and shall have sanctioned the pursuit of peace as we have practiced it, I believe the last sorrow and the final sacrifice of international warfare will have been written.

Let me speak to the maimed and wounded soldiers who are present today, and through them convey to their comrades the gratitude of the Republic for their sacrifices in its defense. A generous country will never forget the services you rendered, and you may hope for a policy under Government that will relieve any maimed successors from taking your places on another such occasion as this.

Our supreme task is the resumption of our onward, normal way. Reconstruction, readjustment, restoration all these must follow. I would like to hasten them. If it will lighten the spirit and add to the resolution with which we take up the task, let me repeat for our Nation, we shall give no people just cause to make war upon us; we hold no national prejudices; we entertain no spirit of revenge; we do not hate; we do not covet; we dream of no conquest, nor boast of armed prowess.

If, despite this attitude, war is again forced upon us, I earnestly hope a way may be found which will unify our individual and collective strength and consecrate all America, materially and spiritually, body and soul, to national defense. I can vision the ideal republic, where every man and woman is called under the flag for assignment to duty for whatever service, military or civic, the individual is best fitted; where we may call to universal service every plant, agency, or facility, all in the sublime sacrifice for country, and not one penny of war profit shall inure to the benefit of private individual, corporation, or combination, but all above the normal shall flow into the defense chest of the Nation. There is something inherently wrong, something out of accord with the ideals of representative democracy, when one portion of our citizenship turns its activities to private gain amid defensive war while another is fighting, sacrificing, or dying for national preservation.

Out of such universal service will come a new unity of spirit and purpose, a new confidence and consecration, which would make our defense impregnable, our triumph assured. Then we should have little or no disorganization of our economic, industrial, and commercial systems at home, no staggering war debts, no swollen fortunes to flout the sacrifices of our soldiers, no excuse for sedition, no pitiable slackerism, no outrage of treason. Envy and jealousy would have no soil for their menacing development, and revolution would be without the passion which engenders it.

Aftermath of the War

A regret for the mistakes of yesterday must not, however, blind us to the tasks of today. War never left such an aftermath. There has been staggering loss of life and measureless wastage of materials. Nations are still groping for return to stable ways. Discouraging indebtedness confronts us like all the war-torn nations, and these obligations must be provided for. No civilization can survive repudiation.

We can reduce the abnormal expenditures, and we will. We can strike at war taxation, and we must. We must face the grim necessity, with full knowledge that the task is to be solved, and we must proceed with a full realization that no statute enacted by man can repeal the inexorable laws of nature. Our most dangerous tendency is to expect too much of government, and at the same time do for it too little. We contemplate the immediate task of putting our public household in order. We need a rigid and yet sane economy, combined with fiscal justice, and it must be attended by individual prudence and thrift, which are so essential to this trying hour and reassuring for the future.

The business world reflects the disturbance of war's reaction. Herein flows the lifeblood of material existence. The economic mechanism is intricate and its parts interdependent, and has suffered the shocks and jars incident to abnormal demands, credit inflations, and price upheavals. The normal balances have been impaired, the channels of distribution have been clogged, the relations of labor and management have been strained. We must seek the readjustment with care and courage. Our people must give and take. Prices must reflect the receding fever of war activities. Perhaps we never shall know the old levels of wages again, because war invariably readjusts compensations, and the necessaries of life will show their inseparable relationship, but we must strive for normalcy to reach stability. All the penalties will not be light, nor evenly distributed. There is no way of making them so. There is no instant step from disorder to order. We must face a condition of grim reality, charge off our losses and start afresh. It is the oldest lesson of civilization. I would like government to do all it can to mitigate; then, in understanding, in mutuality of interest, in concern for the common good, our tasks will be solved. No altered system will work a miracle. Any wild experiment will only add to the confusion. Our best assurance lies in efficient administration of our proven system.

The forward course of the business cycle is unmistakable. Peoples are turning from destruction to production. Industry has sensed the changed order and our own people are turning to resume their normal, onward way. The call is for productive America to go on. I know that Congress and the Administration will favor every wise Government policy to aid the resumption and encourage continued progress.

I speak for administrative efficiency, for lightened tax burdens, for sound commercial practices, for adequate credit facilities, for sympathetic concern for all agricultural problems, for the omission of unnecessary interference of Government with business, for an end to Government's experiment in business, and for more efficient business in Government administration. With all of this must attend a mindfulness of the human side of all activities, so that social, industrial, and economic justice will be squared with the purposes of a righteous people.

With the nation-wide induction of womanhood into our political life, we may count upon her intuitions, her refinements, her intelligence, and her influence to exalt the social order. We count upon her exercise of the full privileges and the performance of the duties of citizenship to speed the attainment of the highest state.

The Role of America

I wish for an America no less alert in guarding against dangers from within than it is watchful against enemies from without. Our fundamental law recognizes no class, no group, no section; there must be none in legislation or administration. The supreme inspiration is the common weal. Humanity hungers for international peace, and we crave it with all mankind. My most reverent prayer for America is for industrial peace, with its rewards, widely and generally distributed, amid the inspirations of equal opportunity. No one justly may deny the equality of opportunity which made us what we are. We have mistaken unpreparedness to embrace it to be a challenge of the reality, and due concern for making all citizens fit for participation will give added strength of citizenship and magnify our achievement.

If revolution insists upon overturning established order, let other peoples make the tragic experiment. There is no place for it in America. When World War threatened civilization we pledged our resources and our lives to its preservation, and when revolution threatens we unfurl the flag of law and order and renew our consecration. Ours is a constitutional freedom where the popular will is the law supreme and minorities are sacredly protected. Our revisions, reformations, and evolutions reflect a deliberate judgment and an orderly progress, and we mean to cure our ills, but never destroy or permit destruction by force.

I had rather submit our industrial controversies to the conference table in advance than to a settlement table after conflict and suffering. The earth is thirsting for the cup of good will, understanding is its fountain source. I would like to acclaim an era of good feeling amid dependable prosperity and all the blessings which attend.

American Trade Must Be Protected

It has been proved again and again that we cannot, while throwing our markets open to the world, maintain American standards of living and opportunity, and hold our industrial eminence in such unequal competition. There is a luring fallacy in the theory of banished barriers of trade, but preserved American standards require our higher production costs to be reflected in our tariffs on imports. Today, as never before, when peoples are seeking trade restoration and expansion, we must adjust our tariffs to the new order. We seek participation in the world's exchanges, because therein lies our way to widened influence and the triumphs of peace. We know full well we cannot sell where we do not buy, and we cannot sell successfully where we do not carry. Opportunity is calling not alone for the restoration, but for a new era in production, transportation and trade. We shall answer it best by meeting the demand of a surpassing home market, by promoting self-reliance in production, and by bidding enterprise, genius, and efficiency to carry our cargoes in American bottoms to the marts of the world.

We would not have an America living within and for herself alone, but we would have her self-reliant, independent, and ever nobler, stronger, and richer. Believing in our higher standards, reared through constitutional liberty and maintained opportunity, we invite the world to the same heights.

But pride in things wrought is no reflex of a completed task. Common welfare is the goal of our national endeavor. Wealth is not inimical to welfare; it ought to be its friendliest agency. There never can be equality of rewards or possessions so long as the human plan contains varied talents and differing degrees of industry and thrift, but ours ought to be a country free from the great blotches of distressed poverty. We ought to find a way to guard against the perils and penalties of unemployment. We want an America of homes, illumined with hope and happiness, where mothers, freed from the necessity for long hours of toil beyond their own doors, may preside as befits the hearthstone of American citizenship. We want the cradle of American childhood rocked under conditions so wholesome and so hopeful that no blight may touch it in its development, and we want to provide that no selfish interest, no material necessity, no lack of opportunity shall prevent the gaining of that education so essential to best citizenship.

Government Must Serve the People

There is no short cut to the making of these ideals into glad realities. The world has witnessed again and again the futility and the mischief of ill-considered remedies for social and economic disorders. But we are mindful today as never before of the friction of modern industrialism, and we must learn its causes and reduce its evil consequences by sober and tested methods. Where genius has made for great possibilities, justice and happiness must be reflected in a greater common welfare.

Service is the supreme commitment of life. I would rejoice to acclaim the era of the Golden Rule and crown it with the autocracy of service. I pledge an administration wherein all the agencies of Government are called to serve, and ever promote an understanding of Government purely as an expression of the popular will.

One cannot stand in this presence and be unmindful of the tremendous responsibility. The world upheaval has added heavily to our tasks. But with the realization comes the surge of high resolve, and there is reassurance in belief in the God-given destiny of our Republic. If I felt that there is to be sole responsibility in the Executive for the America of tomorrow I should shrink from the burden. But here are a hundred million, with common concern and shared responsibility, answerable to God and country. The Republic summons them to their duty, and I invite co-operation.

I accept my part with single-mindedness of purpose and humility of spirit, and implore the favor and guidance of God in His Heaven. With these I am unafraid, and confidently face the future.

I have taken the solemn oath of office on that passage of Holy Writ wherein it is asked: "What doth the Lord require of thee but to do justly, and to love mercy, and to walk humbly with thy God?" This I plight to God and country.

Remembering Fallen Soldiers

Arthur Meighen

Arthur Meighen was a Canadian statesmen who served
twice as Canada's prime minister, from 1920 to 1921 and
again in 1926. On July 3, 1921, he visited Thelus Military Cemetery in Vimy Ridge, France. This was the site of
the Battle of Vimy Ridge, an Allied offensive in which
over ten thousand Canadian soldiers were wounded and
more than three thousand were killed during April and
May 1917. Meighen was at this site for an important occasion: the unveiling of the Cross of Sacrifice, which was
a war memorial dedicated to Canada's fallen soldiers. He
delivered a speech reflecting on the war and the sacrifices
of the soldiers. In addition to honoring the dead,
Meighen states that humankind should repair the devastation caused by the war. He also notes that the world's
task is to learn the lessons of World War I and then to
have the courage to apply those lessons.

T he Great War is past; the war that tried through and
through every quality and mystery of the human mind
and the might of human spirit; the war that closed, we
hoped forever, the long, ghastly story of the arbitrament of
men's differences by force; the last clash and crash of earth's
millions is over now. There can be heard only sporadic conflicts, the moan of prostrate nations, the cries of the bereaved
and desolate, the struggling of exhausted peoples to rise and
stand and move onward. We live among the ruins and the

Arthur Meighen, address at the Thelus Military Cemetery, July 3, 1921.

echoes of Armageddon. Its shadow is receding slowly backward into history.

Honor the Dead

At this time the proper occupation of the living is, first, to honor our heroic dead; next, to repair the havoc, human and material, that surrounds us; and, lastly, to learn aright and apply with courage the lessons of the war.

Here in the heart of Europe we meet to unveil a memorial to our country's dead. In earth which has resounded to the drums and tramplings of many conquests, they rest in the quiet of God's acre with the brave of all the world. At death they sheathed in their hearts the sword of devotion, and now from oft-stricken fields they hold aloft its cross of sacrifice, mutely beckoning those who would share their immortality. No words can add to their fame, nor so long as gratitude holds a place in men's hearts can our forgetfulness be suffered to detract from their renown. For as the war dwarfed by its magnitude all contests of the past, so the wonder of human resource, the splendor of human heroism, reached a height never witnessed before.

Ours we thought prosaic days, when the great causes of earlier times had lost their inspiration, leaving for attainment those things which demanded only the petty passing inconveniences of the hour. And yet the nobility of manhood had but to hear again the summons of duty and honor to make response which shook the world. Danger to the treasury of common things—for common things when challenged are the most sacred of all—danger to these things ever stirred our fathers to action, and it has not lost its appeal to their sons.

France lives and France is free, and Canada is the nobler for her sacrifice to help free France to live. In many hundreds of plots throughout these hills and valleys, all the way from Flanders to Picardy, lie fifty thousand of our dead. Their resting-places have been dedicated to their memory forever by the kindly grateful heart of France, and will be tended and cared for by us in the measure of the love we bear them. Above them are being planted the maples of Canada, in the thought that her sons will rest the better in the shade of trees they knew so well in life. Across the leagues of the Atlantic the heart-strings of our Canadian nation will reach through all time to these graves in France; we shall never let pass away the spirit bequeathed to us by those who fell; "their name liveth for evermore."

Rejecting the New World Order

Adolf Hitler

In 1921 Adolf Hitler became head of the National Socialist (Nazi) Party in Germany. Although he was not the
leader of Germany until 1933, Hitler gave speeches and
spread the National Socialist message throughout the
1920s. The speech that follows was delivered in Munich
on April 13, 1923. In it, Hitler rejects the new world order and the principle behind the League of Nations. International governing bodies, in his view, are not the answer.
Instead, he maintains that struggles between nations are
struggles between the strong and the weak. Hitler's
strongly anti-Semitic views are evident throughout the
speech. He points to Jewish influence as the reason for
America's entry into the war, and he claims that Jewry
seeks to master the world. In addition, he challenges the
notion of "war guilt." The war guilt clause in the Versailles treaty stated that Germany alone was responsible
for World War I. Hitler blames the war on Great Britain's
jealousy of Germany's industrial power. Lastly, Hitler talks
about the need to build a new Germany—a goal that ultimately led to the outbreak of World War II in 1939.

I n our view, the times when there was no 'League of Nations' were far more honorable and more humane. . . .
We ask: 'Must there be wars?' The pacifist answers 'No!'
He proceeds to explain that disputes in the life of peoples are
only the expression of the fact that a class has been oppressed

Adolf Hitler, address in Munich, April 13, 1923.

by the ruling bourgeoisie. When there are in fact differences of opinion between peoples, then these should be brought before a 'Peace Court' for its decision. But he does not answer the question whether the judges of this court of arbitration would have the power to bring the parties before the bar of the court. I believe that an accused ordinarily only appears 'voluntarily' before a court because, if he did not, he would be fetched there.

The League Is Ineffective

I should like to see the nation which would allow itself to be brought before this League of Nations Court in the case of a disagreement without external force. In the life of nations, what in the last resort decides questions is a kind of Judgment Court of God. It may even happen that in case of a dispute between two peoples—both may be in the right. Thus Austria, a people of fifty millions, had most certainly the right to an outlet to the sea. But since in the strip of territory in question the Italian element of the population was in the majority, Italy claimed for herself the 'right of self-determination.'[1] Who yields voluntarily? No one! So the strength which each people possesses decides the day. Always before God and the world the stronger has the right to carry through what he wills.

History proves: He who has not the strength—him the 'right in itself' profits not a whit. A world court without a world police would be a joke. And from what nations of the present League of Nations would then this force be recruited? Perhaps from the ranks of the old German Army? The whole world of nature is a mighty struggle between strength and weakness. An eternal victory of the strong over the weak. There would be nothing but decay in the whole of Nature if this were not so. States which should offend against the elementary law would fall into decay. You need not seek for long to find an example of such moral decay: you can see it in the Reich [Germany] of today. . . .

. . . Before the war two States, Germany and France, had

1. This refers to the territorial disputes between Italy and Austria-Hungary during the war.

to live side by side but only under arms. It is true that the War of 1870–1 meant for Germany the close of an enmity which had endured for centuries, but in France a passionate hatred against Germany was fostered by every means by propaganda in the press, in school textbooks, in theaters, in the cinemas. . . . All the Jewish papers throughout France agitated against Berlin. Here again to seek and to exploit grounds for a conflict is the clearly recognizable effort of world Jewry.

The conflict of interests between Germany and England lay in the economic sphere. Up till 1850 England's position as a World Power was undisputed. British engineers, British trade conquer the world. Germany, owing to greater industry and increased capacity, begins to be a dangerous rival. In a short time those firms which in Germany were in English hands pass into the possession of German industrialists. German industry expands vastly and the products of that industry even in the London market drive out British goods.

The protective measure, the stamp 'Made in Germany,' has the opposite effect from that desired: this 'protective stamp' becomes a highly effective advertisement. The German economic success was not created in Essen alone but by a man who knew that behind economics must stand power, for power alone makes an economic position secure. This power was born upon the battlefields of 1870–71, not in the atmosphere of parliamentary chatter. Forty thousand dead have rendered possible the life of forty millions. When England, in the face of such a Germany as this, threatened to be brought to her knees, then she bethought herself of the last weapon in the armory of international rivalry—violence. A press propaganda on an imposing scale was started as a preparatory measure.

But who is the chief of the whole British press concerned with world trade? One name crystallizes itself out of the rest: Northcliffe[2]—a Jew! . . . A campaign of provocation is carried on with assertions, libels, and promises such as only a Jew can devise, such as only Jewish newspapers would have

2. Born Alfred Harmsworth, Lord Northcliffe (1865–1921) was an influential newspaper publisher in Great Britain.

the effrontery to put before an Aryan people. And then at last 1914: they egg people on: 'Ah, poor violated Belgium! Up! To the rescue of the small nations—for the honor of humanity!' The same lies, the same provocation throughout the entire world! And the success of that provocation the German people can trace grievously enough!

Why America Entered the War

What cause finally had America to enter the war against Germany? With the outbreak of the world war, which Judah had desired so passionately and so long, all the large Jewish firms of the United States began supplying ammunitions. They supplied the European 'war-market' to an extent which perhaps even they themselves had never dreamed of—a gigantic harvest! Yet nothing satisfied the insatiable greed of the Jew. And so the venal press which depended upon the Stock Exchange kings began an unparalleled propaganda campaign. A gigantic organization for newspaper lying was built up. And once more it is a Jewish concern, the Hearst press, which set the tone of the agitation against Germany.

The hatred of these 'Americans' was not directed solely against commercial Germany or against military Germany. It was directed specially against social Germany, because this Germany had up to that time kept itself outside of the principles which governed the world trusts. The old Reich had at least made an honorable attempt to be socially-minded. We had to show for ourselves such an initiative in social institutions as no other country in the wide world could boast. . . . This explains why, even in Germany itself, the 'comrades' under Jewish leadership fought against their own vital interests. This explains the agitation carried on throughout the world under the same watchword.

For this reason the Jewish-democratic press of America had to accomplish its masterpiece—that is to say, it had to drive into the most horrible of all wars a great peace-loving people which was as little concerned in European struggles as it was in the North Pole: America was to intervene 'in defense of civilization,' and the Americans were persuaded so to do by an atrocity propaganda conducted in the name of civilization which from A to Z was a scandalous invention the like of which has never yet been seen—a farrago of lies and forgeries. Because this last State in the world where social aims were being realized had to be destroyed, therefore twenty-six peoples were incited one against the other by this press which is exclusively in the possession of one and the same world people, of one and the same race, and that race on principle the deadly foe of all national States.

Who could have prevented the World War? . . . The German wheel on November 9, 1918, was indeed brought to a standstill. The Social Democratic party in its principal organ, Vorwärts, declared in so many words that it was not in the interest of the workers that Germany should win the war. . . .

Could the Freemasons perhaps stop the war?—this most noble of philanthropic institutions who foretold the good fortune of the people louder than anyone and who at the same time was the principal leader in promoting the war. Who, after all, are the Freemasons? You have to distinguish two grades. To the lower grade in Germany belong the ordinary citizens who through the claptrap which is served up to them can feel themselves to be 'somebodies,' but the responsible authorities are those many-sided folk who can stand any climate, those 300 Rathenaus[3] who all know each other, who guide the history of the world over the heads of Kings and Presidents, those who will undertake any office without scruples, who know how brutally to enslave all peoples— once more the Jews!

Jewish Influence

Why have the Jews been against Germany? That is made quite clear today—proved by countless facts. They use the age-old tactics of the hyena—when fighters are tired out, then go for them! Then make your harvest! In war and revolutions the Jew attained the unattainable. Hundreds of thousands of escaped Orientals become modern 'Europeans.' Times of unrest produce miracles. Before 1914 how long would it have

---

3. "Rathenaus" here means "Jews," in reference to Walther Rathenau, a German Jew who served as Germany's foreign minister.

taken, for instance, in Bavaria before a Galician Jew became—Prime Minister?—Or in Russia before an anarchist from the New York Ghetto, Bronstein ([Leon] Trotsky), became—Dictator? Only a few wars and revolutions—that was enough to put the Jewish people into possession of the red gold and thereby to make them masters of the world.

Before 1914 there were two States above all, Germany and Russia, which prevented the Jew from reaching his goal—the mastery of the world. Here not everything which they already possessed in the Western democracies had fallen to the Jews. Here they were not the sole lords alike in the intellectual and economic life. Here, too, the Parliaments were not yet exclusively instruments of Jewish capital and of the will of the Jew. The German and the genuine Russian had still preserved a certain aloofness from the Jew. In both peoples there still lived the healthy instinct of scorn for the Jew, and there was a real danger that in these monarchies there might one day arise a Frederick the Great, a William I, and that democracy and a parliamentary regime might be sent to the devil.

So the Jews became revolutionaries! The Republic should bring them to wealth and to power. This aim they disguised: they cried 'Down with the monarchies!' 'Enthrone the sovereign people!' I do not know whether today one could venture to call the German or the Russian people 'sovereign.' At least one cannot see any trace of it! What the German people can trace, however, what every day stands in the most crass form before its eyes, is debauchery, gluttony, speculation ruling unchecked, the open mockery of the Jew. . . .

So Russia and Germany had to be overthrown in order that the ancient prophecy might be fulfilled. So the whole world was lashed into fury. So every lie and propaganda agency was brutally set in action against the State of the last—the German—idealists! And thus it was that Judah won the world war. Or would you wish to maintain that the French, the English, or the American 'people' won the war? They, one and all, victors and vanquished are alike defeated: one thing raises itself above them all: the World Stock Exchange which has become the master of the people.

What guilt had Germany herself for the outbreak of the war? Her guilt consisted in this: That at the moment when the

ring closed about her existence Germany neglected to organize her defense with such vigor that through this demonstration of her power either the others, despite their abominable
purposes, would have been robbed of their will to strike, or
else the victory of the reich would have been assured.

The guilt of the German people lies in this: that when in
1912 a criminal Reichstag [German parliament] in its un-
fathomable baseness and folly had refused to allow the raising of three army corps the people did not create for itself
those army corps in the Reichstag's despite. With these additional 120,000 men the Battle of the Marne would have been
won and the issue of the war decided. Two million fewer
German heroes would have sunk into their graves. Who was
it who in 1912 as in 1918 struck its weapons from the hands
of the German people? Who was it that in 1912, as in the last
year of the war, infatuated the German people with his theory that if Germany throws down her arms the whole world
will follow her example—who?—the democratic-Marxist
Jew, who at the same hour incited and still today incites the
others to arm and to subjugate 'barbarous' Germany.

But someone may perhaps yet raise the question whether it
is expedient today to talk about the guilt for the war. Most assuredly we have the duty to talk about it! For the murderers of
our Fatherland who all the years through have betrayed and
sold Germany, they are the same men who, as the November
criminals, have plunged us into the depths of misfortune. We
have the duty to speak since in the near future, when we have
gained power, we shall have the further duty of taking these cre-
ators of ruin, these clouts, these traitors to their State and of
hanging them on the gallows to which they belong. Only let no
one think that in them there has come a change of heart. On the
contrary, these November scoundrels who still are free to go as
they will in our midst, they are, even today, going against us.
From the recognition of the facts comes the will to rise again.
Two millions have remained on the field of battle. They, too,
have their rights and not we, the survivors, alone. There are
millions of orphans, of cripples, of widows in our midst. They,
too, have rights. For the Germany of today not one of them
died, not one of them became a cripple, an orphan, or a widow.
We owe it to these millions that we build a new Germany!

A Common Effort

Gustav Stresemann

Gustav Stresemann was a prominent political leader in Germany's postwar government, the democratic Weimar Republic. As Germany's foreign minister, he suggested that Germany, France, and Belgium should consider the territorial borders determined by the Versailles treaty which concluded World War I to be permanent frontiers. The foreign minister of France, Aristide Briand, agreed with Stresemann's proposal. Seven nations met to discuss these ideas and devised eight agreements addressing territory issues. Germany, France, Belgium, Great Britain, and Italy signed the Treaty of Locarno on December 1, 1925, and Germany was allowed to become a member of the League of Nations. As a result of their diplomatic efforts, Stresemann, Briand, and British secretary of state for foreign affairs, Austen Chamberlain, were awarded the Nobel Peace Prize in 1926.

Stresemann made the following speech in London at the signing of the Treaty of Locarno. He thanks his colleagues at the Locarno conference for their facilitation of productive negotiations and says he views the international cooperative "spirit of Locarno" as a basis for future agreements. He states that it is the will of the countries' leaders to create a new order in Europe, not just the collection of words and clauses, which binds international agreements together. Stresemann acknowledges that World War I resulted in the loss of a generation. He also notes that the war compelled nations to engage in a common effort to ensure peace, and that future generations will regard the postwar world as one of peaceful cooperation.

Gustav Stresemann, address at the signing of the Treaty of Locarno, December 1, 1925.

At the moment when the work begun at Locarno is concluded by our signature in London, I should like to express above all to you, Sir Austen Chamberlain [British secretary of state for foreign affairs], our gratitude for what we owe you in the recognition of your leadership in the work that is completed here today. We had, as you know, no chairman to preside over our negotiations at Locarno. But it is due to the great traditions of your country, which can look back to an experience of many hundred years, that unwritten laws work far better than the form in which man thinks to master events. Thus, the Conference of Locarno, which was so informal, led to a success. That was possible because in you, Sir Austen Chamberlain, we had a leader who by his tact and friendliness, supported by his charming wife, created that atmosphere of personal confidence that may well be regarded as a part of what is meant by the spirit of Locarno. But something else was more important than personal approach, and that was the will, so vigorous in yourself and in us, to bring this work to a conclusion. Hence the joy that you felt like the rest of us, when we came to initial those documents at Locarno. And hence our sincere gratitude to you here today.

In speaking of the work done at Locarno, let me look at it in the light of this idea of form and will. We have all had to face debates on this achievement in our respective Houses of Parliament. Light has been thrown upon it in all directions, and attempts have been made to discover whether there may not be contradictions in this or that clause. In this connection I say one word! I see in Locarno not a juridical structure of political ideas, but the basis of great developments in the future. Statesmen and nations therein proclaim their purpose to prepare the way for the yearnings of humanity after peace and understanding. If the pact were no more than a collection of clauses, it would not hold. The form that it seeks to find for the common life of nations will only become a reality if behind them stands the will to create new conditions in Europe. . . .

I should like to express to you, Herr Briand,[1] my deep

---

1. "Herr" means "Mister" in German. The reference is to Aristide Briand, the French foreign minister who made a speech just prior to Stresemann.

gratitude for what you said about the necessity of the cooperation of all peoples—and especially of those peoples that have endured so much in the past. You started from the idea that every one of us belongs in the first instance to his own country, and should be a good Frenchman, German, Englishman, as being a part of his own people, but that everyone also is a citizen of Europe, pledged to the great cultural idea that finds expression in the concept of our continent. We have a right to speak of a European idea; this Europe of ours has made such vast sacrifices in the Great War, and yet it is faced with the danger of losing, through the effects of that Great War, the position to which it is entitled by tradition and development.

The sacrifices made by our continent in the World War are often measured solely by the material losses and destruction that resulted from the War. Our greatest loss is that a generation has perished from which we cannot tell how much intellect, genius, force of act and will, might have come to maturity, if it had been given to them to live out their lives. But together with the convulsions of the World War one fact has emerged, namely that we are bound to one another by a single and a common fate. If we go down, we go down together; if we are to reach the heights, we do so not by conflict but by common effort.

For this reason, if we believe at all in the future of our peoples, we ought not to live in disunion and enmity, we must join hands in common labour. Only thus will it be possible to lay the foundations for a future of which you, Herr Briand, spoke in words that I can only emphasize, that it must be based on a rivalry of spiritual achievement, not of force. In such co-operation the basis of the future must be sought. The great majority of the German people stands firm for such a peace as this. Relying on this will to peace, we set our signature to this treaty. It is to introduce a new era of co-operation among the nations. It is to close the seven years that followed the War, by a time of real peace, upheld by the will of responsible and far-seeing statesmen, who have shown us the way to such development, and will be supported by their peoples, who know that only in this fashion can prosperity increase. May later generations have cause to bless this day as the beginning of a new era.

Appendix of Biographies

Albert I, king of Belgium (1875–1934)

Born in Brussels, Belgium, Albert became an heir to the throne because his uncle, King Leopold II, had no children. Albert's father and older brother predeceased Leopold II, whose death in 1909 led to Albert's succession to the throne.

Albert received a military education and had a shy, scholarly demeanor. He married a Bavarian (German) princess in 1900, with whom he engaged in such activities as yoga, mountain climbing, and charity work.

When Albert came to the throne in 1909, he faced several challenges. King Leopold II had tarnished the image of the monarchy with harsh policies in the Belgian African colony of Congo. In addition, the very concept of monarchical rule was under attack in Belgium as the Socialist Party pressed for a more republican form of government. Finally, neutral Belgium was located between France and Germany—two countries that became increasingly at odds with each other.

When World War I broke out in August 1914, King Albert I emerged as a strong leader committed to the defense of Belgium's freedom in the face of Germany's invasion. As monarch, Albert was the formal head of the nation's armed forces. Drawing on his education as a soldier and his leadership abilities, the Belgian king led a determined military effort during the war. The queen, for her part, tended to wounded soldiers throughout the war. The king and queen received a warm, respectful welcome in Britain during a visit there in July 1918. In Belgium, they gained the admiration of the country for their wartime leadership, and the nation revealed a renewed appreciation for the monarchy.

After the war, with Belgium prosperous, the king retreated to family life and his prewar hobbies. King Albert I died in a mountain climbing accident in 1934 at the age of fifty-eight.

Newton Baker (1871–1937)

Newton Baker was born in West Virginia to a family with a long southern heritage. He graduated from Johns Hopkins University in 1892 and pursued a law degree at Washington and Lee University.

Baker held a variety of governmental positions. In 1896 he was appointed to the post of secretary to the postmaster general. Two years later he moved to Cleveland, Ohio, to practice law. Baker's speaking ability was noticed by Cleveland's mayor, who made him city solicitor (1902–1912). Baker was an influential member of the mayor's administration, and was elected mayor himself in 1911 and 1913. He acquired a reputation for municipal reform.

In 1916 Baker was appointed secretary of war by President Wilson. He remained in that position until Wilson's second term ended in 1921. Baker had pacifist tendencies, but once the United States entered the war in 1917, he was fully committed to the American effort. An amiable public figure and a fine orator, Baker made a number of prowar speeches to garner popular support for the war. After World War I he was a strong League of Nations supporter.

When his tenure as secretary of war ended in 1921, Baker set up a law practice in Cleveland. He was appointed to the League of Nations World Court in 1928. Baker died on Christmas Day in 1937, leaving behind his wife, a son, and two daughters.

Theobald von Bethmann Hollweg (1856–1921)

A prominent German statesman, Theobald von Bethmann Hollweg was born into a family with an established reputation for agrarian and commercial business. Bethmann Hollweg, however, chose to enter politics, and climbed his way up the Prussian political ladder.

He served as Prussian minister of the interior from 1905 to 1907, and as imperial secretary of state for the interior from 1907 to 1909. In 1909 Kaiser Wilhelm II appointed Bethmann Hollweg imperial chancellor of Germany, and he remained in that position until 1917.

Bethmann Hollweg came into the chancellorship during a time of great political division in Germany. As a modern, open-minded conservative, he was a suitable candidate for bridging political differences between various groups. The chancellor was modestly successful in this regard, but when war broke out in 1914, Germany's political divisiveness was still unresolved.

Bethmann Hollweg also faced challenges in foreign affairs. The naval race between Germany and England, for example, had led to a deterioration in diplomacy. The relations between the two countries were complicated by the influence and demands of the German military. The military's pressure for war in the summer of 1914 thwarted Bethmann Hollweg's attempt to preserve peace. He faced a diplomatic crisis: Austria threatened Serbia with military action if the demands of its ultimatum to hand over most of its ruling autonomy to Austria were not met. In response, Bethmann Hollweg issued a "blank check" of German support to Austria in the event of such measures. This action makes the chancellor one of the leaders responsible for the chain of events that led to World War I.

Throughout the war, Bethmann Hollweg continued to disagree with the military. He never successfully overruled the military leadership on matters of negotiated peace and submarine warfare, and in 1917 he was removed from office. What was in effect a military dictatorship took his place.

Georges Clemenceau (1841–1929)

Georges Clemenceau was a journalist and prominent French statesman. Born and educated in France, he traveled to the United States in 1865 and remained there for four years. While in the United States, he was a correspondent for a Paris newspaper and a teacher at an all-girls school in Connecticut. He married one of his pupils, with whom he had two daughters and one son.

Upon his return to France, Clemenceau was briefly involved in national politics but then served in a variety of municipal positions in Paris. In 1876 Clemenceau resumed his career in the national political arena and was elected to the Chamber of Deputies. He remained in that position until 1893, earning the nickname the "Tiger" for his fierce political style.

Between 1893 and 1903, Clemenceau established himself as a journalist. He wrote for several newspapers and published a novel. His political career was revived with a 1902 election to senator. In 1906 he became premier of France. He remained in office until 1909. He then once again turned to journalism. In 1913 Clemenceau founded a newspaper, *L'Homme libre* (the Free Man), as a vehicle for expressing his views on the "German menace" and armaments.

In 1917, three years after the outbreak of World War I, President Raymond Poincaré asked Clemenceau to serve as prime minister. During his tenure as prime minister, which lasted until 1920, Clemenceau was also minister of war. In addition, he served as president of the Paris Peace Conference (January–June 1919).

Clemenceau ran for president of France in 1920 but was not elected. He then retired from parliamentary politics and devoted his time to writing. In 1929 he died in Paris. His memoirs of World War I and the peace settlement were published posthumously.

Emma Goldman (1869–1940)

Emma Goldman was born to Jewish parents in Kovno, Lithuania. In 1885 Goldman immigrated to the United States. Two years later, she married, divorced, remarried, and separated within a short span of time. In 1889 she began an association with Alexander Berkman, a Russian anarchist.

Goldman and Berkman engaged in radical activism and both served prison sentences. She went to jail for urging the unemployed to steal food; Berkman served time for shooting and wounding a manager who opposed the unionist efforts of workers. The anarchist who shot President William McKinley in 1901 said Emma Goldman's speeches were an influence on him.

During World War I, Goldman was vocal in her opposition to the Conscription Act. She staged numerous protests and anticonscription rallies. In 1917 both Goldman and Berkman were sentenced to two years in prison for having promoted these activities. Goldman's U.S. citizenship was subsequently revoked and she was deported to Russia. Although she supported the Russian Revolution there, she was disappointed by the Bolshevik dictatorship that followed and left Russia.

Goldman married a miner from Wales in order to obtain British citizenship. She wrote three books—two about her disillusionment with Russia and an autobiography. On May 14, 1940, Goldman died in Toronto, Canada. Although she had been banned from entering the United States—with the exception of a ninety-day visit in 1934—her burial in America was permitted. She was laid to rest in Chicago.

Samuel Gompers (1850–1924)

Samuel Gompers was born into a poor family of Dutch Jewish origin in London, England. He received a brief rudimentary education and then served as an apprentice in his father's trade, cigar making.

When Gompers was thirteen, his family immigrated to the tenements of New York City's Lower East Side, where he resumed cigar making. He became active in the local cigar-making union and became its leader. Gompers's experience in this environment as well as his firsthand knowledge of workers' needs helped shape his outlook on unionism.

In 1886 Gompers founded a loose federation of trade unions that ultimately became the American Federation of Labor. The AFL was concerned not with socialist ideals, for which Gompers had little patience, but with the day-to-day material interests of union members. Gompers served as the organization's president every year except one from 1886 to 1924.

Gompers, a well-liked man and a fine public speaker, had good relations with several presidents and was in full support of World War I. He aimed to stop AFL strikes throughout the course of the war; he also spoke out against socialists and pacifists. During the

Paris Peace Conference, Gompers served as president of the International Commission on Labor Legislation.

On December 13, 1924, Samuel Gompers died. His autobiography, *Seventy Years of Life and Labor*, was published in 1925.

Sir Edward Grey (1862–1933)

In 1862 Edward Grey was born into a family with a strong political tradition. He was related to Prime Minister Earl Grey, noted for the Reform Bill of 1832 and for the tea that bears his name. Edward himself became interested in politics and was educated at Winchester and Balliol College in Oxford, England.

In 1892 he was elected to Parliament. That same year he was appointed secretary of foreign affairs, a position he held until 1895; he was appointed a second time in 1905 and served until 1916. Grey served in this position longer than any English politician until that time. As foreign secretary, Grey focused British foreign policy on defending France from an aggressive Germany through a series of secret diplomatic measures.

During the July Crisis of 1914, Britain did not make it clear whether it would support France and Russia or remain neutral. Grey cited "obligations of honor" to France and neutral Belgium as a reason for joining the war on August 4, 1914. His policy led to political party turmoil, and Grey was surprised at the failure of his diplomatic strategy.

Grey was in a challenging position as diplomat, and one of his accomplishments while in office was concluding the Treaty of London (1915), which brought Italy into the war on the side of the Allies. Italy was a prewar ally of Germany and Austria-Hungary but chose to remain neutral upon the outbreak of World War I in the summer of 1914. Grey's persuasion of Italy to join the Allied Powers was considered a great success.

In July 1916, Grey was ennobled as Viscount Grey of Fallodon. Prime Minister David Lloyd George replaced Grey as foreign secretary in December 1916. He then became the leader of the House of Lords. After the war, Grey became the League of Nation's special ambassador to the United States.

Grey wrote two books when his political career came to a close: *Twenty Five Years* (1925) and the popular *The Charm of Birds* (1927).

Warren G. Harding (1865–1923)

Warren Gamaliel Harding was born on a farm in Ohio. He was educated at local schools and graduated from Ohio Central College in 1882. He obtained a job at a local paper and in 1884 he and two partners bought the struggling newspaper *Marion Star*. Harding successfully and skillfully revived the paper.

In 1891 he married a widow. She had one child from her former marriage, but she and Harding had no children of their own.

Harding, a Republican, was involved in local politics and in 1899 was elected to the state senate of Ohio. He served two terms in that position. In 1905 he was elected lieutenant governor but retired two years later. In 1910 Harding made an unsuccessful bid for the governorship.

Harding was elected to the U.S. Senate in 1914. He expressed a probusiness stance. Harding was also a "strong reservationist" on the question of America entering the League of Nations, which means that he was among those senators who were willing to vote for the league only if two conditions were met: the full protection of American sovereignty and the inclusion of the Republicans in drafting the league document.

Harding was a candidate in the 1920 presidential campaign and ran on a postwar "return to normalcy" platform. The likable senator won the largest popular vote yet recorded to become the twenty-ninth U.S. president. Despite his personal popularity, however, Harding was not a strong or capable leader in the office of president. His administration was fraught with scandals, and his own reputation later became tarnished as a result. Harding's health rapidly declined during the summer of 1923. He suffered a heart attack followed by bronchopneumonia while touring the country, and on August 2, 1923, he died.

Gilbert M. Hitchcock (1859–1934)

Born in Omaha, Nebraska, Gilbert M. Hitchcock was educated in local public schools and for two years in Germany. In 1881 he received a law degree from the University of Michigan. He and three partners founded a newspaper in 1885 and four years later expanded the paper through the purchase of another.

A successful newspaper publisher, Hitchcock became interested in politics and was elected to the U.S. House of Representatives in 1902. In 1911 he was elected to the Senate. Hitchcock initially opposed some of President Wilson's wartime measures, and his vote to declare war was cast reluctantly. As World War I progressed, however, Hitchcock became convinced that an international organization was needed in order to secure peace. He became an advocate of the League of Nations and tried to persuade President Wilson to modify certain provisions so that U.S. participation would be more palatable to dissenting senators.

Hitchcock was defeated in his bids for reelection in 1922 and 1930. In 1932 he served as chairman of the Democratic platform committee. He died in Washington, D.C., on February 3, 1934.

Adolf Hitler (1889–1945)

Adolf Hitler was born on April 20, 1889, in Braunau, Austria. His father, with whom he did not get along, died in 1903. Four years later, Hitler took and failed the entrance exam for the Vienna Academy of Art, School of Painting. That same year, 1907, Hitler's mother died. From 1908 to 1913, Hitler was a drifter in Vienna, selling handmade postcards.

Hitler was living in Munich at the outbreak of World War I. During the war, Hitler volunteered for the Bavarian army. He served as a dispatcher, was promoted to lance corporal, and received the Iron Cross for bravery. He was wounded from a gas attack and was recovering in a military hospital when the war ended. He blamed Germany's defeat on the Jews and soon entered politics.

After the war, Hitler used his skill as a public speaker to express his radical anti-Semitic views. He joined a right-wing political party that in 1920 took the name National Socialist German Workers' Party (Nazi). He became the party chairman in 1921.

In November 1923, Hitler staged the Beer Hall Putsch in an unsuccessful attempt to bring down the government. He was sentenced to prison and wrote *Mein Kampf* (My Struggle) during the nine months he was there. Upon his release, he reestablished the National Socialist Party and created a police fighting force for the organization.

Hitler's intention was to overthrow the government by constitutional means. Many Nazis were elected to the legislature in the late 1920s and early 1930s. Hitler ran for president of Germany in 1932 but lost to Paul von Hindenburg, a World War I general. Hitler was appointed chancellor on January 30, 1933.

Hitler's chancellorship soon became a dictatorship, and Germany became a police state. Hitler and the Nazi Party strongly opposed many of the measures of the Treaty of Versailles and began to defy them one by one through rearmament and territorial aggression. The 1930s witnessed increased oppressions of Jews, Gypsies, the handicapped, Communists, homosexuals, and other groups. Their rights as citizens and humans were gradually stripped. When Hitler launched the September 1, 1939, attack on Poland that started World War II, the path was set for the mass killings of the Holocaust. Approximately 11 million people were killed as a result of Hitler's policies; 6 million of them were Jews. Many other millions perished in the war he started.

Aware of the inevitable defeat of Germany, Hitler committed suicide in a bunker on April 30, 1945. The war in Europe ended several days later; it would continue in the Pacific theater until August 10, 1945.

Rudyard Kipling (1865–1936)

Joseph Rudyard Kipling was born to British parents in Bombay, India. Kipling spent his early years in India and was sent to England for his education in 1871. He displayed literary ambitions from his youth and had his first publication of poetry in 1881.

Kipling returned to India in 1882 and wrote numerous newspaper articles and short stories, many of them about British colonial life. He took a lengthy voyage through China, Japan, and the United States in 1889 and found himself acclaimed as a great new author when he reached London.

In 1892 Kipling married and settled in Brattleboro, Vermont, for four happy and prolific years writing poems, short stories, and a novel. He wrote many of his better-known works, such as *Many Inventions, The Jungle Book, The Second Jungle Book*, and *Captains Courageous*, during this time.

The Kiplings settled on the coast of England in 1897. They had two daughters, one of whom died in 1899, and one son, who was killed in World War I. The death of the two children profoundly affected Kipling.

Kipling turned his attention to British imperialism at the close of the nineteenth century. His writings reflect the positive attitude toward imperialism that was popular at the time. However, the eventual criticisms of colonialism led to a decline in Kipling's popularity. He turned to other subjects, such as England's past, and wrote a number of serious, well-received works.

Kipling received the Nobel Prize for literature in 1907, the first British writer to receive this honor. He died in 1936, and his autobiography was published posthumously.

Franklin K. Lane (1864–1921)

Franklin Knight Lane was born in Canada, near Charlottestown, Prince Edward Island. His family moved to California when he was young. Lane received his law degree in San Francisco and practiced law there.

Interested in politics, Lane was a Democrat who ran for governor (1902) and mayor (1903) but lost both races. He was appointed to the Interstate Commerce Commission by President Theodore Roosevelt in 1905 and remained in that position until 1913.

Lane served as secretary of the interior under President Wilson from 1913 to 1920. He was a conservationist who promoted self-government in Alaska (which was not yet an American state) and the increased independence of Native Americans. He also created the National Park Service.

Lane was a popular man whom people said could have been elected president had he not been born in Canada.

David Lloyd George (1863–1945)

David Lloyd George was the son of Welsh parents. When his father died of consumption in 1864, Lloyd George, along with his mother and two siblings, went to live with an uncle. This uncle, named Richard Lloyd, was a preacher and politically active liberal who greatly influenced Lloyd George. This influence characterized David Lloyd George's prominent political career.

Trained as a lawyer, Lloyd George was also an energetic political speaker. He was involved in local politics in the late 1880s. He got married in 1888 and had three daughters and two sons.

The year 1890 marked the first of Lloyd George's fifty-four years in the British Parliament. Domestic affairs were his primary political concern in the years prior to World War I. Lloyd George was appointed chancellor of the exchequer in 1908, where he remained until 1916. In 1915 he also served as minister of munitions under Prime Minister Herbert Henry Asquith. In 1916 he was appointed secretary of war.

David Lloyd George became prime minister of a coalition government in December 1916 after Asquith's resignation. His wartime leadership was marked by energy, determination, an ability to make decisions, and the resolve to end divisiveness. He led the British delegation to the Paris Peace Conference in 1919.

After resigning from the position of prime minister in 1922, Lloyd George remained in Parliament. His influence declined in the years that followed, but he voiced his opinions for the duration of his career. In 1940 Lloyd George declined Prime Minister Winston Churchill's offer to lead a wartime coalition government; he was critical of Churchill's policies on the war. In October 1943, after two years as a widower, Lloyd George remarried. His parliamentary career ended in December 1944, when he resigned for health reasons.

Henry Cabot Lodge (1850–1924)

Henry Cabot Lodge was born to a distinguished family in Boston, Massachusetts. He received his undergraduate, law, and doctorate degrees from Harvard University. His Ph.D. in political science was the first ever granted at Harvard.

Lodge worked as a writer and an assistant editor for several years before entering politics. After two terms as a representative in the Massachusetts legislature, Lodge was elected to the U.S. Congress. From 1887 to 1893, he served in the House of Representatives. For the next thirty years, he was in the Senate.

At the conclusion of World War I, Henry Cabot Lodge favored the imposition of harsh peace treaty terms on Germany. He led a strong opposition to American entry into the League of Nations, fearful that U.S. sovereignty would be compromised. He also opposed ratification of the Treaty of Versailles. In this venture he was successful: The United States never signed the treaty or entered the league. In 1922 Lodge continued to pursue this course of action through his opposition to U.S. membership in the League of Nations's World Court—despite its endorsement by Republican president Harding.

Henry Cabot Lodge died in Boston on November 29, 1924. He left behind one son and one daughter, both of whom had been born to his wife and cousin, Anna Cabot Davis. His other son had died in 1909. Henry Cabot Lodge's account of the League of Nations controversy, *The Senate and the League of Nations*, was published posthumously.

Arthur Meighen (1874–1960)

Arthur Meighen was born in Ontario, Canada, to parents of Irish heritage. He received his education from the University of Toronto and graduated in 1896. For a short while he was a high school teacher, but he soon turned to practicing law in Portage la Prairie, Manitoba, where he got married in 1904.

Meighen, a conservative, was elected to Parliament in 1908 and again in 1911. He was well known for his excellent speaking and debating skills. In 1913 he became Canada's solicitor general. During World War I, Meighen became an even more influential figure and was a leading supporter of conscription and several other controversial wartime measures. In 1917 he was appointed secretary of the state and then minister of the interior.

Meighen served as prime minister of Canada from July 1920 to December 1921. He remained in politics until 1926 and then retired from public life to pursue other interests.

In 1932 Meighen returned to politics and became the government leader in the Senate until 1935. He accepted the leadership of the Conservative Party during World War II but was defeated in a 1942 election. Meighen died on August 5, 1960, in Toronto.

Nicholas II, czar of Russia (1868–1918)

Nicholas II, the son of Alexander III, was born into Russia's Romanov dynasty. He was educated by private tutors, spoke several languages, and traveled extensively, including an around-the-world voyage in 1890–1891. Although he was heir to the throne, Nicholas II had little interest or involvement in politics before becoming the czar (emperor). Nicholas II became czar on October 20, 1894. A month later, he married a German princess, with whom he had four daughters and one son, who was a sickly boy. The czar and czarina enjoyed a close, loving marriage, and Nicholas seemed more devoted to family life than to affairs of the state.

The autocratic monarchy of Russia was in decline as the nineteenth century came to a close. Viewed by many statesmen as out of touch with the masses and in need of reform, the governmental institutions of Russia did not successfully meet the challenges of the modern world in the early twentieth century. Thus, when World War I began in the summer of 1914, the monarchy was a lingering but unstable political structure. During the war, when Nicholas II was commanding troops, internal political strife flourished. A revolution broke out in February 1917.

On March 15, 1917, Nicholas II abdicated the throne in favor of his brother Michael, who refused to become emperor. Thus, Nicholas's peaceful abdication marked the end of the Romanov dynasty's rule, which had lasted over three hundred years.

The imperial family was forced to Siberia in the summer of 1917. In July 1918, they were murdered by the Bolsheviks, a revolutionary Communist group that had come to power in October 1917. Their bodies were unearthed from a forest in 1991, following the Soviet Union's collapse. On July 17, 1998, Nicholas II, his wife, three of their daughters, and four servants received a proper burial in St. Petersburg, eighty years after they were killed.

George W. Norris (1861–1944)

Born on a farm in Ohio, George William Norris received his undergraduate and law degrees from Valparaiso University. Upon becoming a lawyer, he taught school and served as a clerk in a local law office. He then moved to Nebraska, where he set up a law practice in 1899.

Norris, a Republican, was elected county prosecutor in 1892 and district judge in 1895. In 1902 he was elected to the U.S. House of Representatives, where he served until his 1913 election to the Senate. Norris opposed much of President Woodrow Wilson's domestic and foreign policies and voted against the declaration of war on Germany in 1917. He also opposed American participation in the League of Nations.

Senator Norris was the leading force behind the Twentieth Amendment to the Constitution (1933), which regulated the frequency with which Congress met and changed the presidential inauguration from March to January. He was also a key figure in Nebraska's adoption of a unicameral legislature. Nebraska is the only U.S. state to structure its legislature in this manner.

Norris supported only limited American intervention in Europe in the years prior to World War II. He became an independent in 1936 and won reelection. He was defeated, however, in 1942.

Raymond Poincaré (1860–1934)

Born in Lorraine, future French president Raymond Poincaré was the son of a meteorologist and civil servant. He was educated in Bar-le-Duc and Paris, and he studied law at the Sorbonne.

Poincaré served in the Department of Agriculture and was elected deputy for the Meuse region of France. From 1890 to 1899, he served in a variety of cabinet positions for several presidents. Between 1899 and 1912, Poincaré held just one cabinet post, serving as minister of finance in 1906. The rest of his time was devoted to his successful law practice and a position in the Senate.

Poincaré was the premier of France four times: 1912, 1922–1924, 1928, and 1928–1929. In 1913 he was elected president of France, and he remained in that position until January 1920. In the summer of 1914, Poincaré urged Russia, a French ally, to delay mobilization in order to prevent further escalation of the tension between Russia and Germany and Austria-Hungary. Russia mobilized anyway, and Germany declared war on Russia on August 1, and on France two days later.

Throughout World War I, Poincaré worked to sustain the morale of the French soldiers and citizens. He visited the front lines, hospitals, and training camps. In November 1917, Poincaré put aside his political rivalry with Georges Clemenceau and called on the capable leader to form the president's cabinet. This ability to put state interests before personal feelings was a successful tactic for maintaining political unity in France during the war. Poincaré was a strong president who firmly defended France's interests at the Paris Peace Conference in 1919.

After his presidency, Poincaré held several governmental positions until 1929. Between 1926 and 1930 he penned his multivolume memoirs chronicling the years 1911 to 1920. He was offered a fifth premiership in 1930 but declined. Poincaré died on October 15, 1934, in Paris.

Gustav Stresemann (1878–1929)

Gustav Stresemann, the son of a small businessman, was born in Berlin, Germany, in 1878. His experience in the family business prompted Stresemann to study economics, as well as political science, at the University of Berlin, where he obtained his doctorate.

In 1907 and again in 1914, Stresemann was elected to the Reichstag (German parliament). During World War I, he expressed support for Germany's monarchy and annexationist policies. He became chairman of the National Liberal Party in 1917. After the war and the establishment of the democratic Weimar Republic, he founded the German People's Party. His goal was to restore Germany to a position of international respect while repairing relationships with former enemy countries.

Stresemann became foreign minister of the Weimar Republic in 1923, and he served briefly as chancellor that same year. While in the position of foreign minister, Stresemann ended the occupation of the Ruhr, defended Germany's acceptance of the Treaty of Versailles, and worked to revise reparations payments and border disputes. He and French foreign minister Aristide Briand were awarded the 1926 Nobel Peace Prize for fostering a cooperative postwar spirit.

Stresemann died of a stroke on October 3, 1929, in Berlin.

William Howard Taft (1857–1930)

William Howard Taft, the son of a judge, was born in Ohio. Taft graduated second in his class of 121 at Yale University and was a well-respected member of the student body. He received his law degree from Cincinnati Law School in 1880. Taft was married in 1886, and in this happy marriage he and his wife had two sons and a daughter.

Taft held a number of prominent positions in politics and law. He served in several public offices in Ohio and became a superior court judge in 1887. President Benjamin Harrison appointed Taft to the position of U.S. solicitor general in 1892. That same year,

Harrison nominated him for a seat on the Sixth Federal Circuit Court of Appeals in Ohio.

Taft then held a new and unexpected post. In the aftermath of the Spanish-American War, President William McKinley appointed him to be the first civil governor of the Philippine Islands in 1901. He remained in that position until he took office as President Theodore Roosevelt's secretary of war in 1904. Taft was responsible for the construction of the Panama Canal. He and President Roosevelt became close friends, and in 1908 Roosevelt endorsed Taft as the Republican presidential candidate.

Taft served one term as president of the United States, but he was never comfortable in politics and endured much criticism while in office. After his presidential term he accepted a law professorship at Yale. In 1921 Taft's lifelong dream came true when President Warren G. Harding appointed him chief justice of the Supreme Court. Content in this position, Taft sat on the Supreme Court until his death on March 8, 1930.

Wilhelm II, kaiser of Germany (1859–1941)

Wilhelm II, Germany's last monarch, traced his royal lineage to three ruling families. He was born into the Prussian Hohenzollern dynasty and was also a descendant of Russia's Catherine the Great (ruled 1762–1796). In addition, Wilhelm II's maternal grandmother was Britain's Queen Victoria (ruled 1837–1901). Wilhelm was born with a left arm deformity that, though mild, made him self-conscious throughout his life.

Wilhelm was educated at the University of Bonn but left after two years to enter the military. A good marksman, Wilhelm enjoyed military life and the traditions of the Prussian army. Many Prussian officers were members of the conservative aristocracy. The Prussian army and aristocracy generally disliked liberal-minded England, and this attitude influenced Wilhelm's own perception of that country.

In 1881 he married a German princess, with whom he had six sons and two daughters. When the reigning monarch died in March 1888, Wilhelm II's father, Friedrich III, became kaiser (king). However, his reign lasted only ninety-nine days, during which time he fell into a coma and died of cancer of the larynx. Wilhelm II then ascended the throne at age twenty-nine.

Even though Kaiser Wilhelm II lacked experience as a leader, he demanded unwavering devotion from those who surrounded him. In 1890 he dismissed Chancellor Otto von Bismarck, who had overseen the creation of the German kingdom in 1871 and whose powerful persona threatened Wilhelm II. According to both diplomats and those within Wilhelm II's inner circle, Wilhelm possessed personality traits such as rudeness, tactlessness, and insensitivity that made him a difficult ruler to deal with. He is also remembered as an inept ruler.

In the years prior to World War I, Wilhelm II made a number of diplomatic blunders and seemingly aggressive overtures, such as devising military preparations for war and building up a vast German navy to rival England's. Yet despite his martial tendencies, Wilhelm II was reluctant to engage in a European-wide conflict when World War I broke out in the summer of 1914. He was hoping to limit the struggle between Austria and Serbia. When alliances were upheld and war seemed inevitable, Germany faced enemies on both the eastern and western fronts.

Throughout the war, Wilhelm II played a relatively minor role in decision making and strategy. As the war came to an end, Germany brewed with revolution, and many people wanted a republic instead of a monarchy. It was in this atmosphere that Wilhelm II abdicated the throne on November 9, 1918. He fled in exile to Holland, remarried in 1922, and ended his days there in solitude.

Woodrow Wilson (1856–1924)

Woodrow Wilson was the son of a well-educated, successful Presbyterian pastor with a forceful personality. Wilson's father exerted a good deal of influence on the future American president, and Wilson became a man of strong convictions.

Wilson was highly educated, having received a law degree from the University of Virginia (1881) and a Ph.D. from Johns Hopkins University (1886). In 1885 Wilson married and had three daughters. He practiced law for a while and then pursued a career in academia. He taught at Princeton, published his writings on history and government, and served as president of Princeton University from 1902 to 1910. Wilson remained interested in political life, however, and was elected governor of New Jersey in 1911. He held that position until 1912, when he was elected to be the twenty-eighth president of the United States. Wilson became a widower in 1914 and remarried in late 1915. He was reelected president in 1916.

World War I defined Wilson's presidency. Initially declaring a policy of American neutrality upon the outbreak of war in Europe during the summer of 1914, Wilson urged Congress to declare war on Germany in 1917. Several events led to Wilson's change in attitude. One was the deliberate sinking of the British passenger liner *Lusitania* by a German submarine in 1915, after which Germany rescinded its policy of unrestricted submarine warfare. Another incident was the interception of the Zimmermann telegram, a communication from Germany to Mexico that attempted to persuade Mexico to side with Germany against the United States. The final event that brought America into the war was Germany's decision to return to a policy of unrestricted submarine warfare. Wilson said the Americans entered the war as associates of the Allies in April 1917 in order "to make the world safe for democracy."

When the war ended on November 11, 1918, nations turned their attention toward a peace settlement. Wilson spearheaded the peace process and established his "Fourteen Points," which were his goals for a just peace. One of the points was a proposal for the creation of a League of Nations, an international arbitration organization designed to prevent future wars. The idea for the league was controversial, however, and the United States never joined the organization; it also never ratified the Treaty of Versailles, which provided for it.

In September 1919, shortly after making a speech to rally support for the League of Nations, Wilson suffered a massive stroke. He was incapacitated for the rest of his term, which ended in March 1921, and remained an invalid until his death in 1924.

Chronology

1914

June 28: Austria-Hungary's Archduke Franz Ferdinand and his wife, Sophie, are assassinated during a visit to Sarajevo, Bosnia, by Gavrilo Princip of the Serbian anarchist group Black Hand.

July 5: Germany informs its ally, Austria-Hungary, that it will support whatever action Austria-Hungary chooses to take against Serbia.

July 23: Austria-Hungary sends an ultimatum to Serbia, making fifteen demands and threatening military action if the demands are not met.

July 24: Serbia appeals to Russia for help in the situation with Austria-Hungary.

July 28: Austria-Hungary declares war on Serbia.

July 31: Russia, a supporter of Serbia, orders a general mobilization of its army.

August 1: In response to the mobilization, Germany declares war on Russia. Germany sends an ultimatum to Belgium asking to send soldiers through neutral Belgian territory. Belgium rejects the ultimatum.

August 3: Germany declares war on France, Russia's ally.

August 4: Germany invades neutral Belgium. Great Britain declares war on Germany; this is in response to Germany's war against Great Britain's allies, France and Russia, and to Germany's violation of Belgian neutrality. President Woodrow Wilson of the United States declares American neutrality.

August 12: Austria-Hungary invades Serbia.

August 23: Japan declares war on Germany.

September 6–12: The First Battle of the Marne ensues. In this battle the French, with British help, halt a swift German advance. Germany's retreat leads to a stalemate and trench warfare. Both France and Germany suffered approximately

250,000 casualties. Over 12,700 British casualties were incurred as well.

October 29: Turkey enters the war on the side of Germany and Austria-Hungary.

December 25: Soldiers along the western front call an unofficial Christmas truce and the fighting ceases. Some soldiers even exchanged gifts with their enemies in no-man's-land, the open territory dividing enemy trenches.

1915

May 7: The British passenger liner *Lusitania* is sunk by a German U-boat. The death toll is 1,198 people, including 128 American civilians.

May 23: Italy declares war on its prewar ally, Austria-Hungary.

1916

February 21–December 18: The Battle of Verdun, the longest battle in World War I, is fought. This German offensive was intended to "bleed the French white," in the words of German general Erich von Falkenhayn. Heavy casualties were suffered on both sides: about 550,000 for France and about 434,000 for Germany.

May 4: Germany renounces its policy of unrestricted submarine warfare.

May 31–June 1: The Battle of Jutland, between the British and German naval forces, is fought. It is the longest battle in naval history. There are over sixty-one hundred British casualties and over twenty-five hundred German casualties.

June 4–September 20: Russia launches the Brusilov Offensive against Austria-Hungary, which lost (including prisoners of war) 1.5 million soldiers. Following the Brusilov Offensive, Romania enters the war on the side of the Allies.

July 1–November 18: The Battle of the Somme. This British offensive was a response to the Battle of Verdun and incurred the greatest number of casualties in England's military history—about 420,000. Casualties for France were 200,000 and for Germany, an estimated 500,000.

August 28: Italy declares war on Germany.

August 31: Germany halts submarine attacks.

October 15: Germany resumes submarine attacks.

December 12: Germany issues a peace proposal suggesting a compromise peace. It is not accepted.

1917
February 1: The German High Command resumes unrestricted submarine warfare.

February 3: The United States severs its diplomatic ties to Germany as a response to the unrestricted submarine warfare policy.

February 24: The British government intercepts a telegram from German foreign minister Arthur Zimmermann to the Mexican government. The telegram proposes a German-Mexican alliance against the United States.

March–November: Russia undergoes revolution. First, there is a provisional government in power. Then, the Bolsheviks, a Communist political party, take over and remain in power.

March 1: The Zimmermann telegram is published in the American press.

March 15: Czar Nicholas II of Russia abdicates the throne. He is the last czar to rule Russia.

March 20: President Wilson's war cabinet votes in unanimous support of a declaration of war on Germany.

April 2: President Wilson delivers his war message to the U.S. Congress.

April 6: The United States declares war on Germany.

June 27: Greece joins the war on the side of the Allies.

July 31–November 6: The Battle of Passchendaele (the Third Battle of Ypres), a British offensive launched by Sir Douglas Haig, was the war's last battle of tremendous attrition. The British suffered about 310,000 casualties and the Germans, about 260,000. The Allies gained several kilometers in the front as a result.

December 7: The United States declares war on Austria-Hungary.

1918

March 3: Soviet Russia concludes a separate peace with Germany. The agreement is called the Treaty of Brest-Litovsk.

October 3 and 4: Germany and Austria-Hungary submit peace notes to President Wilson asking for an armistice.

October 21: Germany ends unrestricted submarine warfare.

October 30: Turkey concludes an armistice with the Allies.

November 3: Austria-Hungary concludes an armistice with the Allies.

November 7–11: Germany and the Allies negotiate an armistice.

November 9: Kaiser Wilhelm II of Germany abdicates and flees to Holland the next day.

November 10: The German Republic is founded.

November 11: The fight of the Great War ends at 11 A.M.

1919

January 18: The Paris Peace Conference begins.

May 7–June 28: The Treaty of Versailles is drafted and signed. The Paris Peace Conference ends.

For Further Research

Books

RICHARD BESSEL, *Germany After World War I*. Oxford: Clarendon, 1993.

ROGER CHICKERING, *Imperial Germany and the Great War*. New York: Cambridge University Press, 1998.

DEBORAH COHEN, *The War Come Home: Disabled Veterans in Britain and Germany, 1914–1939*. Berkeley and Los Angeles: University of California Press, 2001.

JOHN MILTON COOPER JR., *Breaking the Heart of the World: Woodrow Wilson and the Fight for the League of Nations*. New York: Cambridge University Press, 2001.

MODRIS EKSTEINS, *Rites of Spring: The Great War and the Birth of the Modern Age*. New York: Anchor Books, 1990.

DAVID M. ESPOSITO, *The Legacy of Woodrow Wilson: American War Aims in World War I*. Westport, CT: Praeger, 1996.

BYRON FARWELL, *Over There: The United States in the Great War, 1917–1918*. New York: Norton, 1999.

NIALL FERGUSON, *The Pity of War: Explaining World War I*. New York: Basic Books, 1999.

MARTIN GILBERT, *The First World War: A Complete History*. New York: H. Holt, 1994.

ERIK GOLDSTEIN, *The First World War Peace Settlements, 1919–1925*. New York: Longman, 2002.

ROBERT GRAVES, *Good-bye to All That: An Autobiography*. New York: Anchor Books, 1998.

EDWYN GRAY, *The U-Boat War, 1914–1918*. London: Leo Cooper, 1994.

RUTH HENIG, *The Origins of the First World War*. New York: Routledge, 2002.

DAVID G. HERRMANN, *The Arming of Europe and the Making of the First World War*. Princeton, NJ: Princeton University Press, 1996.

HOLGER H. HERWIG, *The First World War: Germany and Austria-Hungary, 1914–1918*. New York: St. Martin's, 1997.

A.A. HOEHLING, *The Great War at Sea: A History of Naval Action, 1914–1918*. New York: Barnes and Noble, 1995.

MICHAEL HOWARD, *The First World War*. New York: Oxford University Press, 2002.

ERNST JÜNGER, *The Storm of Steel: From the Diary of a German Storm-Troop Officer on the Western Front*. New York: H. Fertig, 1996.

JOHN KEEGAN, *The First World War*. New York: Random House, 1999.

JENNIFER D. KEENE, *The United States and the First World War*. New York: Longman, 2000.

W. BRUCE LINCOLN, *Passage Through Armageddon: The Russians in War and Revolution, 1914–1918*. Westport, CT: Praeger, 1996.

MARGARET MACMILLAN, *Paris 1919: Six Months That Changed the World*. New York: Random House, 2002.

GARY MEAD, *The Doughboys: America and the First World War*. New York: Overlook, 2000.

DAVID RAMSAY, *"Lusitania": Saga and Myth*. New York: Norton, 2002.

MICHAEL E. SHAY, *A Grateful Heart: The History of a World War I Field Hospital*. Westport, CT: Greenwood, 2002.

HEW STRACHAN, ED., *World War I: A History*. New York: Oxford University Press, 1998.

BARBARA TUCHMAN, *The Guns of August.* New York: Macmillan, 1962.

———, *The Zimmermann Telegram.* New York: Viking, 1958.

SPENCER C. TUCKER, *The Great War, 1914–1918.* Bloomington: Indiana University Press, 1998.

JONATHAN F. VANCE, *Death So Noble: Memory, Meaning, and the First World War.* Vancouver: University of British Columbia Press, 1997.

ROBERT WELDON WHALEN, *Bitter Wounds: German Victims of the Great War, 1914–1939.* Ithaca, NY: Cornell University Press, 1984.

JOHN W. WHEELER-BENNETT, *Brest-Litovsk, the Forgotten Peace, March 1918.* New York: Norton, 1971.

JAY WINTER, *The Great War and the British People.* Cambridge, MA: Harvard University Press, 1986.

JAY WINTER AND JEAN-LOUIS ROBERT, EDS., *Capital Cities at War: Paris, London, Berlin, 1914–1919.* New York: Cambridge University Press, 1997.

ROBERT WOHL, *The Generation of 1914.* Cambridge, MA: Harvard University Press, 1979.

ROBERT ZIEGER, *America's Great War: World War I and the American Experience.* Lanham, MD: Rowman & Littlefield, 2000.

Websites

ENCYCLOPAEDIA OF WORLD WAR ONE, SPARTACUS EDUCATIONAL HOME PAGE, www.spartacus.schoolnet.co.uk/FWW.htm. This segment of the Spartacus Educational teaching history website, which provides online tools for teaching history, features a chronology of events, identifications of key figures and battles, excerpts from primary documents, and links to other World War I sites.

FIRST WORLD WAR.COM, www.firstworldwar.com. A multimedia history of World War I. This is an extensive site that employs primary and secondary documents, photos, and video and audio recordings to convey the history of the war from a number of perspectives, from military battles to songs from the home front.

World War I Document Archive, www.lib.byu.edu/~rdh/ wwi. This Brigham Young University site contains primary documents relevant to World War I. Documents from all nations participating in the war are included on this site. Links to other World War I sites are also available.

Index